D1189860

Max Weber's Political Ideas
in the Perspective
of Our Time

German Information Center

MAX WEBER

Max Weber's Political Ideas
in the Perspective
of Our Time

by Karl Loewenstein

Translated from the German
by Richard and Clara Winston

The University of Massachusetts Press · 1966

Copyright © 1965 Athenäum Verlag GmbH., Frankfurt am Main
Copyright © 1966 by The University of Massachusetts Press

Library of Congress Catalog Card Number 66-16541
Printed in the United States of America

*Gratefully remembering
Heidelberg, as it was
when the author was young*

Foreword

In the decades since Max Weber's death in 1920, many scholars have mined the rich deposits of his *oeuvre*. His most significant achievements—the theory of social and economic organization, the sociology of religion and of law, the methodology of philosophy and the humanities—have received the attention they merit. Nor has the part Max Weber played in German politics during the last years of his life been overlooked. One aspect of his work, however, seems to have been given somewhat less than its due. This is the significant contribution which he made as an intellectual leader to German policy of his day and of the future during and just after the First World War. His extensive treatises on these issues contained his political thinking on the state and constitution, his real ideas on the theory and practice of politics. Students of Weber may have dismissed these works as no more than journalistic by-products of his mind—of high quality, to be sure, like everything he did, but still journalism outraced by history, which therefore has been rightly consigned to oblivion. Possibly this approach explains the one glaring gap in the general appreciation of his work.

In these pages I have undertaken to rectify this situation. For Max Weber viewed what were then the burning problems of Germany's political reconstruction in the context of political organization throughout the Western world. In so doing he gave the problems a significance that transcended the topical occasion by far. The problems of Germany provided Weber, as a thinker and a system-builder, with a welcome opportunity to show the Germans that their own political problems reflected fundamental problems of political organization common to the whole Western world. Consequently, what he wrote on German politics of the day constituted a contribution to political theory, and remains as topical as ever. It seems a rewarding task to examine his ideas critically and in context, all the more so since apparently no one has yet undertaken such a study.

I have attempted to interpret Max Weber's political ideas on their own terms, as it were; that is to say, as they appeared to him at the time he expounded them. I therefore let Max Weber speak for himself. Even were I more familiar with the subsequent literature on Max Weber than I am, since I have not lived in Germany for more than thirty years, I would prefer to omit any consideration of such secondary materials and keep the learned apparatus of footnotes to a minimum.

A pure and simple account of Max Weber's political and constitutional theories as of the second decade of this century would at best be of limited historical interest today. His political analyses become of real significance to us if we pose them against the developments that have changed the face of the world in the interceding years. Some of these developments have deepened the lines Weber drew, others have blurred them. In pointing out the road we have traveled in the interval, my discussion will, I hope, help clarify the governmental and constitutional problems of our own day. For more detail I must refer the reader to my book, *Political Power and the Governmental Process* (Chicago, 1957; Phoenix Paperback, 1965), which treats the contemporary scene in a fuller context.

Some sections of this essay are based on a lecture I delivered on June 9, 1964, at the University of Munich as part of a lecture series celebrating the one hundredth anniversary of Weber's birth.

KARL LOEWENSTEIN

Contents

I. Remarks on Method

1. Max Weber's Typology of Patterns of Government in Historical Perspective

Although limited in scope, the frame of reference of our undertaking is the history of ideas. I shall attempt to appraise the validity, in the light of our present experience with contemporary political forms and procedures, of Max Weber's ideas on the organization of the political process and the technique of statecraft. This latter term is Max Weber's own.[1] It denotes all the institutions, procedures and modes of conduct associated with the operations of government in the incipient mass society of Max Weber's day, as well as in the full-blown technological mass society of today. It focuses attention especially upon those forms of organization that have developed in the Western world, since it was with these ideas that Max Weber was principally concerned.

What we are attempting in the present essay, then, is both a study of foresight and a study in retrospect. For the first, we must reconstruct the background of experience and state of knowledge against which Max Weber projected his thoughts about the future shape of Western state society. In retrospect, on the other hand, we shall have to measure Max Weber's views

---

[1] See, for example, Max Weber, *Gesammelte politische Schriften* (Tübingen: Mohr, 1958) (hereafter cited as *Pol. Schr.*), pp. 296 ff.

against the new ways of manipulating the machinery of the state that have developed during the past half-century.

Methodologically, our project is in some ways parallel to certain studies of Alexis de Tocqueville which are attracting considerable interest nowadays. More than a century ago, when mass democracy was only in its infancy, de Tocqueville traveled through the United States. The recent studies seek to evaluate de Tocqueville, not only as a keen-eyed tourist, but as a prophet with a well-nigh uncanny sense of the shape of things to come in America's present-day democratic society.

Such a comparison between de Tocqueville and Max Weber does all honor to the former. As a conscious empiricist, however, the Frenchman is really not in the same class with the German systematizer, whose knowledge of political and social matters was truly universal. In this respect Max Weber towers over the leading sociologists and social psychologists of the nineteenth and twentieth centuries—such men as Lorenz von Stein, Auguste Comte, Graham Wallas, Gaëtano Mosca, and Vilfredo Pareto. In originality and wealth of ideas, only Jacob Burckhardt might possibly be mentioned in the same breath with Weber. But Burckhardt's field of vision began and ended with Europe; he equated the history of Europe with "world history." Max Weber's researches, on the contrary, took in the historical tides of the entire globe.

Both in his scope and his insight into the operations of history, Max Weber properly belongs in the class of Montesquieu, whose *Esprit des Lois* is the first truly comprehensive work of political sociology in the modern age. But in one important aspect, the retired French magistrate cannot equal the retired German professor; that is, in the latter's historical knowledge, which remains to this day—and indeed especially in this day of ours—almost inconceivable. Along with that vast knowledge, moreover, Weber had the gift of organizing the results of his researches into generally relevant categories or types, and thereby rendering it practically useful. For Weber was the last polyhistor to date: a universal scholar of Aristotelian proportions. He was as much at home in the Egypt of the New Kingdom, in republican Rome, in ancient Judaism, in medieval feudalism, and in the Oriental cultures of India and China as he was in the Germany, England, America, France, and Russia of his own day.

Because he systematized his historical insights within a framework of "ideal types," he was also better equipped than anyone else to classify the social phenomena of the past. For their bewildering variety he found permanently meaningful categories. He was also able to fit the experiences of his own time into his universal framework and could, therefore, venture to make scientific predictions of future developments on the basis of his general system. If he regarded his system as beyond challenge, his conviction was by no means a piece of cranky scholarly arrogance. Rather, his typology was based on so vast a body of learning, so great a mass of data, that he could not help considering it universally valid. And indeed one of his basic conclusions (startling to his contemporaries, and nowadays taken for granted) was—and this, we may add, was one of his primary concerns throughout—"In the simple questions of the technique of arriving at policy decisions, the mass state does not permit unlimited choice. There are only a restricted number of forms."[2]

Drawing upon historical experience, he compiled what he felt to be an all-inclusive list of possible forms of political organization or "types of governance." From these categories he derived parallels for the present and perhaps even conclusions about the future. Our purpose now, in the very spirit of Weber, is to reverse the process and to examine in retrospect how good Weber's prognoses were.

A reservation is in order. Max Weber, like Alexis de Tocqueville before him, had not thought of assuming the mantle of the

---

[2] *Pol. Schr.*, pp. 296 ff.

prophet. In the final analysis Weber was also an observing empiricist—with the added virtue that, unlike the Frenchman, he was able to fuse his historical analysis into a typological system. His approach was non-valuational; his observations were never intended to lead to a chiliastic salvationism in the vein of Arnold Toynbee, nor to a pessimistic vision of cyclical decline à la Oswald Spengler. Before we begin our retrospect, we must, in all fairness, make the point that in Weber's day there was not even the faintest glimmering of those revolutionary upheavals which the machinery of state would undergo in the technological mass society. Not even the most imaginative science fiction novelist could have foreseen those. It is therefore neither just nor sensible to try to give Weber good or bad marks for bull's-eyes or misses on this issue. The value of our retrospect lies rather in showing to what extent the prognoses he derived from his historical typology have been borne out in our time. In undertaking this task, we shall be able to measure how far we have come since Max Weber's day in rationalizing the political process and its mechanisms. To arrive at such a picture would represent an added reward for our labors.

2. Max Weber as a Political Scientist

In fairness to Weber, and in keeping with our aims, we must begin by examining the special conditions of the age in which Max Weber formed his political views. Our study is based chiefly on his political writings dealing with current events in his Germany.[3] They were all, let us not forget, *livres d'occasion*,

---

[3] These are collected in *Pol. Schr.* and include principally (in chronological order): "Wahlrecht und Demokratie in Deutschland" (1917), pp. 133 ff.; "Parliament und Regierung im neugeordneten Deutschland" (1918), pp. 294 ff.; "Deutschlands künftige Staatsform" (1918), pp. 436 ff.; and that still exemplary essay, "Politik als Beruf," pp. 439 ff. Johannes Winckelmann, who is generally credited with doing so much for Weber studies, has attempted to assemble the apposite material in

though of major caliber. All were written toward the end of the
First World War or in the chaotic first year of the Weimar Republic. They were produced, in other words, at a time when the
Imperial Reich was on the verge of collapse. Bismarck's deter-
mination to make Germany a Greater Prussia had imposed a
heritage upon the country which proved to be all but unbearable,
and one which the disaster of defeat had erased. On the other
hand, Weber was also writing at a time when authority was
generally discredited and the old attitudes of subservience were
being shattered. This meant that Germany was being offered a
rare chance to turn over a new leaf in her history. She now had
the opportunity to seek salvation in a Western and European,
rather than a "German" *Staatsidee,* which Weber, for his part,
persistently denounced. Germany, he believed, should adopt the
well-tested political techniques of the practically advanced Western world. This, however, was not to be until our own era, when
the Bonn government succeeded the unfortunate experiments of
Weimar and the Hitler regime—a fact that may lend topical interest to the present study.

I need not belabor the point that sociology as Max Weber
practiced it was the *scientia universalis* within which all other
branches of the humanities could lodge. Within that framework,
studies in political and constitutional law as the infrastructure of
rational politics were not undertaken for their own sake, but
only as a means to a sociological end. Max Weber was, it is

Staatssoziologie (Berlin: Duncker & Humblet, 1956). This collection
also contains the typology of governmental authority, under the title,
"Die drei reinen Typen der legitimen Herrschaft" (*Staatssoziologie,* pp.
99 ff.). I have also referred upon occasion to the general material in
Wirtschaft und Gesellschaft (4th ed., Tübingen: Mohr, 1956), hereafter cited as *W.u.G.*

A cautionary *avis au lecteur* is in order here. Our study is no exercise
in "Weberology." That is, we have attempted to interpret Max Weber
in terms of his total context, in the "spirit" of his political writings,
without citing chapter and verse in every single case for the opinions
ascribed to him.

true, a lawyer by training and, in addition, a favorite pupil of the great Mommsen. Nevertheless, the professorships he held were in the field of political economy. Yet he could have taught constitutional law with the sovereign command of a specialist in that field.[4] His knowledge of the law of England, the United States, Russia, and to some extent of France and Switzerland—in addition to that of Germany—was amazing in breadth and depth. This is all the more remarkable when we consider that at that time neither comparative law nor political science as such was taught at German universities.

Inevitably, given his deep identification with the plight of his fatherland, Max Weber's basic approach as a political publicist was Germanocentric. But it was in the nature of his thought that he had to occupy himself with German affairs as specific aspects of his general sociological typology. It was from this angle that he judged his country's current history. To the casual observer it may have seemed that he was only taking his stand on the politics of the day. But the universal systematizer of political and social phenomena was always looking over the commentator's shoulder. And from our present vantage point we see that the scholar in the long run eclipsed the politician. Therefore, his political commentary holds its attraction and its interest for us, even where it has been outmoded by subsequent and especially by present-day realities.

Unlike the present-day popularizers of history in the guise of

---

[4] See, e.g., his masterly analysis of the situation and the consequences that flowed from the noted and notorious Article 9, Section 2 of the Bismarck constitution of 1871 (*Pol. Schr.,* pp. 330 ff., 408 ff.). The article prohibited concurrent membership in the Bundesrat and the Reichstag, thereby automatically excluding the Reich Chancellor and the leading Reich cabinet ministers from the Reich parliament. This one measure was tantamount to nullifying the principle of the parliamentary system, the only feasible form of democratic government for Germany. This stumbling block was only removed at the eleventh hour, by the constitutional amendment of October 28, 1918 (*Reichsgesetzblatt,* p. 1274).

scholars, Max Weber had no illusions about the fate of the true scholar's work. In his deservedly famous lecture, *Wissenschaft als Beruf*,[5] he comments, not resignedly but with a certain definite pride: "A work of art that is a true consummation is never surpassed, never becomes obsolete. Conversely, those of us who work as scholars know that what we have done will be obsolete in ten, twenty, or fifty years. This is the fate and is indeed the meaning of scientific work. . . . Every scientific achievement poses new questions, and its very purpose is to be surpassed and to become outmoded." Weber was a scholar and nothing else; he never wanted to be an amateur magician. Although he happened to be a genius, who can blame him—as a scholar—for failing to foresee the ills which the Pandora's box of the next half-century would loose upon the world?

3. *The Twentieth-Century Revolution in Political Technique*

This, then, is our problem: how does the world of government and politics appear in the second third of the twentieth century, when matched against the political ideas so brilliant an observer as Max Weber was able to conceive at the end of the First World War? Today it is as if we are living in another universe. In the nineteenth century, progress and reason were seen as complementary. Thanks to progress, rationality was coming more and more to be the ruling principle of human conduct, especially in the realm of politics. That century of optimism was blown sky-high by the guns of August 1914. The twentieth century may indeed have brought progress, if we take the word to mean technical improvements in the externals of our standard of living. But the political process is no longer guided by reason. Instead of being complementary, progress and reason have actually become antithetical. Rational motivation of community life has given

---

[5] Reprinted in *Wissenschaftslehre* (Tübingen: Mohr, 1951). Quotation from p. 634.

way to mass emotionality, which even the rational individual can rarely and only imperfectly escape—for he too is a member of the masses, and conformity has become the watchword of the age. Mankind has been subjected to the totalitarian state, a form of society permeated by coercion rather than by the principle of rational utility which guided the nineteenth-century state. The totalitarian state, whatever ideology it may assume for justification, is the legalization of illegal violence. It operates by conjuring up an illusion of spontaneous emotional responses on the part of the masses, while in reality the masses have been forced into acquiescence by a host of crude as well as subtle techniques.

After the First World War, constitutional democracy[6] seemed to many of the best minds the infallible key to a happier future for the nations. But its seemingly promising springtime proved to be only a fleeting Indian summer. Today, constitutional democracy has been forced on the defensive throughout the world. To put that fact in Max Weber's language: the illegitimate governance by violence of plebiscitary Caesarism has ceased to be a historical exception and has become a common phenomenon. This term denotes a pattern of rule in which a single individual, carried to power by the confidence of the emotionalized masses, assumes supreme command. In the past, government by established rule or by sacred tradition* predominated; only once in a while would a dictator rise to power on a wave of mass emotion. Now Caesarism, wearing the pseudo-legal mask of neo-presidentialism, or else appearing as naked military dictatorship, has become ubiquitous. The dynamism of multiparty systems, based on free decisions, has been replaced by the coercive apparatus of the one-party state. Radio and television—in Max Weber's day still

---

[6] For the terminology employed here, see generally Karl Loewenstein, *Political Power and the Governmental Process* (Chicago, 1957; Phoenix Paperback, 1965).

* Weber's expressions are *Herrschaft kraft Satzung* and *traditionale Herrschaft*.

hidden in the future along with atomic energy, supersonic air-planes, and automation—have made the past's naive methods of propaganda and opinion-molding as antiquated as the horse and buggy. Both the fascist and the communist brands of totalitari-anism have imposed the coercive ideology of the state party upon the self-determination of the free individual. When the state assumes control over the means of production and distribution, that capitalistic free enterprise which Max Weber regarded as "a system necessarily dominating the economy, and through it the daily lives of men,"[7] has become extinguished. Nowadays, more than one-third of the world's population lives under such non-capitalistic regimes. Another large segment of the human race has to live under military dictatorships which either deck them-selves out with a few ideological ribbons or govern by simple brute force, with no pretense to any ideology. The constitutional state, then restricted to Western Europe and America, has been formally espoused in Asia and Africa but has not really struck root there. And even in the West, the social goal has ceased to be the individual's free integration into his community. Rather, political reality is shaped by an all-embracing welfare state that assures its citizens a degree of economic security beyond all pre-vious expectations but concomitantly regiments and devours them.

In retrospect, the First World War appears but the prelude to a second and even more terrible conflict. Total exhaustion in total war has been followed by an unprecedented and perhaps, in the long run, deceptive general prosperity, at least for the nations of the West. In the course of this universal rise in living standards, something has quietly developed that has not, amid the hurly-burly of current events, received anything like the un-derstanding it deserves. The implacably contradictory ideologies of Max Weber's day have been defused, so to speak. They have

---

[7] *Pol. Schr.*, p. 242.

given way to a universal ideology to which the masses in all nations are attached with blind devotion: the craving for a better
standard of living. No matter whether a country is organized on
the basis of liberal capitalism, socialism, totalitarian communism
or fascism, its government defines its supreme aim as the achievement of better material life for its people.

On this score, Max Weber was a generation and more ahead
of his time. For he was completely indifferent to the standard
ideologies of his day, which were principally liberal capitalism
and socialism—totalitarian communism and fascism not yet having made their appearances. When he called for "socialization,"
he meant a technical improvement of the machinery of state;
socialism was in no sense an absolute value. In a world gripped
by an inexorable bureaucratization, ideologies as philosophies
shaping the conduct of public and private life seemed of the
smallest consequence to him.[8] In taking this indifferent view toward the various ideologies, in regarding them as wholly rela-
tive attitudes toward society conditioned by time and environment, Weber was leaping over half a century and setting both
feet squarely in our own time. For anyone at all keen at reading
the signs of our times must recognize that the ideological fronts
dividing the world have become largely effaced. Whatever their
labels, all ideologies of the present day come down to questions
of how and at what pace the standard of living of the masses can
be improved. The dispute in both camps—and neither of the two
is coherent nowadays—rages solely around the means of achiev-
ing the universal ideology. Is free enterprise, which even in the
liberal states has long since ceased to be free, or total socialization, or a system that finds some mean between the public and

---

[8] It is significant that Max Weber nowhere speaks of "ideologies" as
coherent philosophical systems. The nearest he comes to the matter is
in his use of the word "ideologues" (e.g., *Pol. Schr.*, pp. 55, 355, and
passim), which he obviously equates with intellectuals.

private sectors of the economy best suited to accomplish the end in view? That is the overriding question.

The altered position of the individual in society may well be linked with this leveling of ideologies. For along with the withering of the ideologies has gone a general weakening of the idealism that sustained and fructified them. The individual is concerned solely with securing the best place for himself and his family in a community which he hopes will remain static. Since everyone is better off than before, the individual feels no need to reform society as a whole, let alone to revolutionize it. The class struggle, too, has been left behind on the deserted ideological battlefield of our grandfathers, Max Weber's contemporaries. The idealism that seeks to throw off the burden of historical injustice may still exist, here and there, among underdeveloped peoples or socially underprivileged groups as one of the aftereffects of colonial rule; but it no longer prevails in the satiated West and in the not quite satiated but by now far from hungry East.

Finally, general prosperity and the welfare state have had another important effect. To Max Weber and his time, the highest virtue of a citizen in a democratic state-society was the individual's concern with his own government. But that concern has been largely blunted; instead, there is a lethargy that in many places is not even resignation. The masses obediently go to the polls when told to, but on the whole they leave political action to the professional politicians, just as Max Weber foresaw.[9] One outward sign of this political apathy is the decrease in registered party members, observable in all countries. There is nothing surprising about the trend, for the generation that followed Max Weber's went through too much in the way of inflation and devaluation, economic insecurity, revolution and war. It

---

[9] See *Pol. Schr., passim,* especially pp. 377 ff.; this subject also forms the core of *"Politik als Beruf,"* pp. 509 ff.

simply lacks the fiber to subordinate personal well-being to the general welfare.

One might go on and on listing the radical changes in political goals and in political techniques that have taken place since Max Weber's day. Even such a master of historical typology as Weber could not possibly have foreseen them all. In the following pages we shall attempt to show how close to present-day realities he nevertheless came in many of his predictions.

II. Max Weber's View of the Political Future of Germany

It is impossible to neatly separate Max Weber's prognosis for Germany's political future from his general predictions. Many of the problems posed by the defeat of Germany overlap the broader questions of democratic, constitutional government. Since, however, German affairs were his primary concern, let us briefly consider them first.

1. Attitude toward Monarchy

Max Weber was an unabashed monarchist, both by family tradition—his parents were National Liberals—and by personal preference. Before the collapse of 1918, he considered monarchy, on grounds of tradition and continuity, the logical form of government for Germany. He also saw it as desirable for reasons of political utility: "The highest official position in the state is definitely occupied and therefore withdrawn from the political struggle for power."[1] Such thinking was altogether in the spirit of the nineteenth century, when the monarch could and did claim an active part in political leadership. Max Weber was thinking especially of the realm of foreign policy. He had been deeply impressed by the quiet work behind the scenes of Edward VII of England—"more than any other monarch of recent times a

---

[1] Thus frequently, e.g., *Pol. Schr.*, p. 325.

dominant personality."[2] He had no great opinion of the powe
of the crown to act as a check upon the German bureaucrac
and rightly so. For the unpurged, still monarchistic German bu
reaucracy was instrumental in sabotaging the Weimar Republi

Despite Weber's generally favorable attitude toward monarch
as an institution, he was no admirer of the wearer of the Ge
man crown, Kaiser Wilhelm II. On the contrary, he was ou
raged by the conduct of this last of the Hohenzollerns durin
his reign, and especially after the collapse. Instead of consentin
to a timely abdication, and thus, outwardly at least, assumin
some of the blame for the disaster, the Kaiser dodged respons
bility by fleeing to neutral Holland. In so doing, he sealed th
fate of the dynasties of the *Länder,* whose role as patrons o
culture, especially in the smaller princely courts, made the
passing, in Weber's view, a regrettable loss to Germany. On th
other hand, Weber had nothing but contempt for the way var
ous dukes and princes in the midst of the war had haggle
among themselves over royal and ducal titles to lands in th
occupied but still not conquered East.

It must have come hard to this convinced monarchist to er
dorse the parliamentary republic. Even after the collapse, he co
tinued to assert that parliamentary monarchy was "technical
the most adaptable and therefore the strongest form of gover
ment."[3] But since the dynasties had exhausted their usefulne
as elements of political integration, no alternative existed but
parliamentary republic. Moreover, it seemed to Weber that th
various dynasties could make no contribution to the new feder
union that had to be established. He had little faith in th
prospects of restoring the monarchy. And, in fact, in due cour
the monarchistic spirit perished so completely among the Ge

---

[2] See *Pol. Schr.,* pp. 198, 316, 421. Most recent research, howeve
attributes far less influence to him; see Philip M. Magnus, *King Edwa
the Seventh* (London: Murray, 1964).

[3] See *Pol. Schr.,* pp. 437 ff.

mans that, except for Austria, no movement for such restoration ever arose.

If, however, we look at the matter from our present-day perspective, we see that Max Weber's opinion about monarchy as a socially and politically integrating institution was altogether correct. In the seven western European countries where monarchy has held its ground, it proved to be far more firmly established than anyone could have predicted a generation ago.[4] Even in England, where the monarch in normal times has been considered a decorative and rather expensive figurehead in the bow of the ship of state, the crown plays a not altogether negligible part behind the scenes as a balancing factor between the two parties. Its usefulness to foreign policy, however, has vanished completely. Almost every one of the remaining dynasties has faced severe trials of strength in the course of the past several decades: the abdication of Edward VIII in England in 1936, of Leopold III of Belgium in 1950, and the domestic strains in the Dutch royal family. But in general, monarchy in western Europe has gained stability in the intervening years.[5] Certainly we may say that Max Weber's confidence in its strictly limited usefulness has not been discredited by events.

2. Max Weber and the Weimar Constitution

Weber's part in the shaping of the Weimar Republic's constitution is so well known[6] that we need only outline it briefly. The distrust of provincial party bosses kept him out of the National Assembly itself. But his writings on the issues were widely

---

[4] This does not, however, apply to the fickle Greeks, who since 1920 have repeatedly expelled their monarch and might do so again.

[5] On monarchy in general after the Second World War, see Karl Loewenstein, *Die Monarchie im modernen Staat* (Frankfurt am Main: Metzner, 1952).

[6] See, e.g., J. P. Mayer, *Max Weber and German Politics* (London, 1944; 2nd ed., Faber & Faber, 1946), pp. 93 ff.; R. Petzke, *Max Weber und sein Einfluss auf die Reichsverfassung* (Leipzig, 1925).

read, and policy-devising committees welcomed his expert advice. Since many of the proposals and suggestions he made in his writings on Germany's future were already in the air, they were also taken up by others. But he had the ear of Hugo Preuss, the architect of the Weimar Constitution. Weber strongly advocated a parliamentary system that would do away with Bismarck's burdensome legacy: Prussian hegemony in the Reich. As it turned out, this measure probably went much further than Weber had expected. Perhaps the Bismarck Constitution had not been intended to effect so thorough a "Prussification of the Reich" as had actually resulted from it. But except for the South German states, that was its result. Under the Weimar Constitution the process was reversed. There took place a "federalization of Prussia," produced above all by the splitting of the votes for the Reichsrat assigned to Prussia as a whole among her various provinces (Art. 63, Sec. 1, Par. 2).

Furthermore, Weber made a strong and decisive plea for a popularly elected Reich president.[7] He considered a strong president the indispensable counterweight to a party-dominated parliament. With wise foresight, he also recommended a safeguard against any abuse of the presidential powers. This was incorporated into Article 43, Section 2 of the Constitution, which provided for recall of the president by Reichstag and people. But his influence was also reflected in some of the lesser provisions, such as the rule in Article 24, Section 1 permitting a parliamentary investigating committee to be established on the motion of a minority of the deputies to the Reichstag. It was also due to his writings that the constitution included provisions for initiative and referendum (Arts. 72 ff.).[8]

Max Weber's plea for a popularly elected president subsequently became a matter for violent controversy. To Weber him-

---

[7] See, e.g., the essay "Der Reichspräsident" (February, 1919), in *Pol. Schr.*, pp. 480 ff.

[8] See below, pp. 52 ff.

self, it was patent that the role of such a president would be quite different from that of the president of the United States, since the American Congress was not a parliament in the accepted sense. But Weber was in no way responsible for the most fatal mistake in the Weimar Constitution: to wit, the coupling of the presidential power to appoint and dismiss the chancellor with the requirement that the chancellor must at the same time enjoy the confidence of the Reichstag. To anyone with a knowledge of western parliamentarism it would have seemed monstrous that a chancellor who still had the confidence of the Reichstag, or who at any rate had not forfeited it by losing a formal vote of confidence, could be arbitrarily dismissed by a president who did not like his policies—as was to happen to Bruening in May 1932. Naturally, Weber cannot be blamed for the perversion of the parliamentary government that inevitably followed from that constitutional flaw: the "presidial" cabinets towards the end of the Weimar Republic. These cabinets, responsible to the president instead of the parliament, made it only too easy for the Austrian corporal to seize the reins of government. But events in France in our own time confirm Max Weber's political theories about the basic need for a plebiscitary head of state. Caught up in one of its recurrent plebiscitary periods, France, too, has shifted from a president elected by parliament and possessing no power to a popularly elected chief of state who is the center of all power.[9]

The proposal for yoking a popularly elected president with a popularly elected parliament sounded reasonable at that time. But in retrospect we perceive that the idea was an unfortunate mistake from the standpoint of political realities. For when conflicts arose between these two political organs, both anointed with

---

[9] On Max Weber's presumable attitude toward General de Gaulle, see Karl Loewenstein, "Max Weber als 'Ahnherr' des plebiscitären Führerstaats," in *Kölner Zeitschrift für Soziologie und Sozialpsychologie*, vol. 13 (1961), pp. 286 f.

the oil of democracy, one proved stronger than the other. The elected executive was an individual and therefore more effective in the decision-making process than the parliament, hampered as it was by numbers and by party divisions. Even before Max Weber's time, the Second French Republic of 1848 had proved that point: within three years the popularly elected president, Louis Napoleon, was able to outmaneuver the National Assembly and seize dictatorial powers. Weimar and the Spanish Republic under the constitution of 1931, which was modeled on Weimar, produced the same impasse and the same results. In the de Gaulle constitution of 1958, on the contrary, the danger of such conflict was forestalled by establishing the presidency as an independent center of political power. Since the amendment to the French Constitution of 1962, the president is elected directly by the people. An oppositional parliament can, at most, obstruct the president's wishes; under no circumstances can it make him subservient to itself.

3. German Federalism

Max Weber viewed the organization of relationships between the central government and the individual member states—which is what we mean by federalism[10]—as a uniquely German problem, although he cited American, Swiss, and Canadian parallels. Here was one of the cases where his foresight best proved itself; and although his practical influence had long since faded, it indirectly helped shape the federal structure of the Bonn government. Weber decided that a centralistic or unitarian solution would not do for Germany, this in spite of the fact that he was an advocate of socialization, which required a strong central power. Socialization was only tentatively undertaken in the Weimar Republic, and Weimar's Article 165a and, even more so,

---

[10] See principally *Pol. Schr.*, pp. 406 ff., 440 ff.

Article 15 of the Bonn Constitution* remained dead letters. He had already foreseen[11] that in the period after the defeat of 1918 the Allies would never tolerate a centralized Germany, so that the Republic had no choice but to be federalistic. Such an attitude on the part of the victors was even more marked after the Second World War. The Americans especially, in that respect much more naive than their allies, insisted on integral federalism because they considered German centralism *fons et origo malorum* of the Hitler dictatorship. They utterly failed to understand the fact that the Hitler movement had used the smaller states as springboards from which to attack Prussia and the Reich. In any case, in view of the overriding force of German particularism, Weber assumed that the new government would have to be cast in a federalistic mold. His chief concern, then, was with the federal organ through which the states would participate in the decisions and the administration of the German state as a whole. In other words, which type of federal organ was to be preferred: one consisting of delegates of the *Länder* governments or of representatives of the *Länder* people?[12] As it turned out, the German tradition did not fail to reassert itself. The American device of electing senators by popular vote rather than through the state legislature was then relatively new (XVIIth Amendment, 1913), but Weber felt that it would not suit German conditions, given the intensity of German particularism. Equally unacceptable was the privileged position of Prussia under the Bismarck Constitution. Therefore he settled for the traditional solution: deputies to the Reichsrat appointed by the state governments and acting according to the instructions received from them. The Reichsrat would thus remain an executive instrument of the state governments. The dynamics of party politics within it would be determined by the constellation

---

[11] *Pol. Schr.*, p. 449.
[12] *Pol. Schr.*, p. 450.
* The German term is "Basic Law."

of parties in each state. Weimar, and Bonn also, adopted this scheme.

Perhaps there might have been a chance after 1945 to change over to the American system of popular election of the members of the Bundesrat (as the Reichsrat is called in the new Germany). The Bundesrat would then have served as a genuine upper house, instead of remaining a house representing only the states. Certainly the preconditions for such a change existed. The state of Prussia had been wiped out by a rude stroke of the pen on the part of the Allied Control Commission (February 1946). The full historical import of that act has never been adequately grasped, let alone discussed. It remains an open question whether a man like Max Weber would have approved of it; he fought Prussian hegemony with all his might, but he had an appreciation of the genuine values of real Prussianism. Weber, who considered Bismarck's legacy as it was embodied in the Constitution of the Reich a misfortune for the whole of Germany, could not know, could not even guess, that what Bismarck had built up would be annihilated by Hitler and Hitler's defeat. But the elimination of Prussia opened the way for the creation of fewer, economically more viable territorial entities in a country whose population had become largely homogeneous, and which was freed at last from feudal junkerdom. The American pattern, by which the people of the states were represented in an upper house, would therefore have been quite feasible. But the state governments, so unexpectedly strengthened after the 1945 collapse, refused to let the Bundesrat slip from their control. They had no desire to surrender their own instrument of power to the vagaries of party-dominated popular elections. Moreover, Bonn lacked one of the vital mechanisms by which centralism can oppose extreme federalism, and had done so under both the Bismarck and Weimar Constitutions—namely, a federal bureaucracy. Thus the typically German version of federalism—a chamber, in this case the Bundesrat, composed of representatives of governments rather than of the people—came to the fore once again. In this matter, too, Max Weber had predicted rightly.

More clearly than anyone else in his day, Weber recognized that the key element of every federal government was not the method of federal decision-making, but the question of federal finances.[13] "The financial relationships are what most decisively determine the real structure in a federal government."[14] Weimar, following the pattern of the Bismarck Constitution, found a rather centralistic solution, appropriate to the broader powers of the central government: a federal income tax formed the core of its financial system. But where a federal income tax skims the cream, territorial units are forced onto so lean a diet that we can no longer speak of genuine federalism. Such has been the lesson of financial experience. Under the Bonn Constitution, with its extremely states'-rights bent, the financial problem has been only provisionally settled, on an emergency and patchwork basis (Arts. 105 ff.). That is plainly demonstrated by the recurrent tug of war over finances, with the federal government always demanding a larger share in the taxes. The Swiss Federal Government likewise suffers from this chronic illness of temporary, stopgap solutions for its financial needs. Should present prosperity decline or vanish entirely, serious imbalances would probably develop in both countries.

Max Weber also foresaw the imperative need for territorial reorganization within Germany[15]—the issue the Weimar Republic called Reich reform. Many of the dwarf states inherited from the Bismarck Constitution in fact had to "end their senseless existence," as he had urged, by amalgamation (Thuringia) or absorption (Koburg by Bavaria). The hegemony of Prussia was broken by the well-known two-fifths clause of Article 61, Section 1, Paragraph 2ᵈ, and by transfer of half its votes in the Reichsrat to the provincial authorities (ibid., Par. 2). Bonn car-

13 *Pol. Schr.*, p. 468.
14 *Ibid.*
15 *Pol. Schr.*, pp. 450 f.

ried through the work that Weimar had imperfectly begun—
thanks in part to the changes already wrought by Nazi central
ism and in large part to the sometimes unwise but ultimatel
beneficial territorial regroupments imposed by the occupying
Allied Powers. Only ten states (with West Berlin, eleven) hav
remained, and the Federal Republic has thereby become a mor
homogeneous and compact governmental structure than eithe
Bismarck's Reich or the Weimar Republic ever was. The advo
cates of reunification prefer to overlook the fact that the loss o
the East helped bring this about. To realize the importance o
this factor, we need only imagine the shifts in economic and po
litical equilibrium that would inevitably result if Germany wer
restored to her frontiers of 1937.

Finally, there is one more development which, if not directl
predicted by Max Weber, does bear out his theory that economi
conditions determine the modern state: the Federal Republic
although it has conscientiously tried to conform to the rituals o
federalism, has had to resort to centralism much more than eve
the Weimar Republic. For under the conditions of the moder
technological mass society, the really relevant decisions in ever
federal state—this applies not only to Germany—are made o
the federal, not on the state level. Major economic and socia
policies can only emanate from the central government. No coun
try can afford to let these things be determined by the dubiou
"sovereignty" of the member states. Max Weber clearly foresav
that with the growth of the technological mass society, federalisn
has become less and less viable as an organizing principle. H
considered this an inescapable consequence of universal suffrage
And despite all the protestations of the stalwart federalists, thi
phenomenon of a declining federalism and, correspondingly, o
a strengthened centralism, may be seen as a world-wide phe
nomenon.[16]

---

[16] See Karl Loewenstein, *Political Power and the Governmental Proc
ess*, pp. 292 ff.

III. Max Weber's
View of Political Reality
after World War I

1. Over-all View

Before and after the end of the First World War, Weber published a number of essays dealing specifically with the political future of Germany. Nevertheless, they reflect his general view of the political situation in Western governments and his ideas concerning it. We may sum up his insights as follows:

Democracy, as Weber saw it, was a postulate of practical reason devoid of emotional overtones. Nowhere did Weber idealize or ideologize; nowhere did he assert that democracy is the "best" form of government, that it accords with human nature and dignity, or eulogize in a similar vein. He believed in democracy because there was no reasonable alternative to it. At least from the German viewpoint, integral democracy appeared to him the only feasible way to overcome authoritarianism, and thus to attain civic liberty in place of previous subservience to non-elected power holders. It is also significant that nowhere in his work do we find a discussion of freedom as a metaphysical or ethical value. Weber himself, a free personality in thought and action, took it for granted;[1] but he evidently did not think much of free-

---

[1] Cf. his remark in *Pol. Schr.*, p. 321: "For after all it is primitive self-deception to imagine that we today (even the most conservative among us) would be able to live without these achievements dating from the period of 'the rights of man.'" The context of this sentence is Weber's comment on the danger: "How is it *possible at all* in the face

dom as an ideological abstraction. Where he speaks of freedom, he treats it as a mode of sociological conduct conditioned by coexistence in a particular environment.[2] The contemporary reader is bound to wonder at the lack of emphasis Weber placed upon the postulates of freedom that are everywhere the center of concern in our time: human rights as the standard of human conduct and social justice as the ultimate purpose of state action. Weber thought little of a natural law, superior to the State, as that term was conceived in 1776 or 1789 or even as it was modified in 1848 to suit the outlook of the bourgeoisie.[3] Those who regard democracy as an essential realization of liberty, or even only the guarantor of liberty, will scarcely hail Weber as a convinced democrat. For he conceived of freedom and democracy as not necessarily identical—in fact, far from it, often antithetical. In this respect his attitude rather resembles that of de Tocqueville, who coined that classical slogan of the "tyranny of the majority." But to blame Weber on that score is to overlook the fact that basically he took freedom for granted, and in keeping with the ideas of the nineteenth century felt that its only prospect of

---

of this tendency toward bureaucratization to preserve *any* remnants of 'individualistic freedom of mobility' in *any* sense?" (Italics in original.)

[2] See, e.g., "Politik als Beruf" (*Pol. Schr.*, p. 501). There Weber speaks of the "so-called free societies . . . free not in the sense of freedom from domination by violence, but in the sense of there being no traditionally legitimized . . . power of sovereigns as the exclusive source of all political authority."

[3] The only pertinent treatment of "freedoms" in *W.u.G.*, vol. II, p. 733 has an exclusively sociological orientation; there Weber traces freedom of conscience, as the basic freedom, to religious sectarianism. Nowhere in the *Pol. Schr.* is there a full discussion of freedoms as supreme values. When the words "free" and "freedom" appear, they are often in quotation marks, to suggest that they are meant only conditionally. References to freedom in Weber's earlier writings on the Russian situation show a similar slant. The infrequency of such references in his tables of contents, which are otherwise fairly complete, suggests that as a scholar Max Weber was interested in the phenomenon of freedom only in the sociological sense, not in freedom as an ethical value.

realization was a humanly decent political order. Such an order, he believed, could arise only out of rational techniques of statecraft. What mattered, then, were the institutions such statecraft would create. Ethical protestations in themselves were only superfluous rhetoric.

In the light of German conditions, he concluded that lack of freedom sprang from the dominance of an all-powerful bureaucracy. Democratization was the only alternative to the stranglehold of authority. He took an entirely pragmatic viewpoint, with no concessions to the illusions of ideology. Liberty, he believed, could be secured by specific techniques and institutions that gave the people the means to check and restrain an overbearing bureaucracy. He viewed "parliamentarization" as the best of such instruments, since the monarchy was incapable of performing this task. By parliamentarization he meant more than the mere existence of a political institution that could be called a parliament. If, like the Reichstag created by Bismarck, such a body was without the effective constitutional means for influencing the executive, all it had was the "will to impotence." What Weber envisaged was a form of genuine popular representation based on *universal suffrage,* whereby the millions of citizens could participate in political decision-making. He was aware, of course, that the British Parliament, even without universal suffrage, had served splendidly as such an instrument down to the twentieth century. Nevertheless, its pattern seemed to him no longer in tune with the times, and he considered universal suffrage the demand of the hour. Yet he never postulated parliamentarism as an end in itself, or as an ideal in itself desirable. Rather, along with its usefulness as a check upon the bureaucracy, he saw it as the spawning ground best suited for political leadership. This was to him a problem of primary importance, to which a parliament seemed to hold the answer. Out of the free dynamics of partisan politics, within the framework of the parliamentary process, an elite leadership would arise. Parliamentarization and the selection of the leadership, therefore, were complementary. Universal suffrage and parliamentary process necessitate the formation of *political parties*. Parties mobilize the masses of the electorate and organize the elected representatives of the people into effective cadres capable of action within the parliament. Political parties, to Weber, were freely competitive and freely recruiting associations founded on voluntary membership. He was not averse on principle to the proposals for an *upper house,* or a second, coordinate chamber of deputies; but he was strongly opposed to any plan for electing such a second house on an occupational-group basis.

Democratization of the commonwealth was, to Weber, the essential correlate of genuine parliamentarism. Since a republican Germany had become inevitable, he would have it implemented by devices of *direct democracy*. With a fully modern vision, he included in this form of democracy not only the referendum and the initiative but also direct popular election of the head of state. He considered such institutions not only as valuable (though not infallible) regulators and correctives of representative government but as valid manifestations of the will of the sovereign people.

As things looked then in Germany, these prerequisites of parliamentarization were certain to be achieved. But he had few illusions about the practical results of integral democratization in a modern mass society. The natural type of political organization in such a society is *Caesarism,* the rise of the leader who, by the magic of his personality and mission, emerges as the chosen spokesman for the enfranchised masses and holds that position as long as he proves his worth. According to Weber's typology of forms of governance, plebiscitary democracy would be a fount of political leadership, which was as valid as the kind of leadership to arise out of parliamentarism under the rule of a leisure class. If one signal element of Max Weber's political theory is predominant, it is the central question of *political leadership.*

As far as he was concerned, all other technical aspects of statecraft are secondary to this.

We have summarized the principal elements of Max Weber's political sociology with some accuracy, we hope, although someone else might place the accents differently. We shall now attempt to analyze these elements one by one in terms of Weber's forecast and our present knowledge.

2. The Franchise

Before the collapse in 1918, Max Weber persistently denounced the moral injustice and political folly of the Prussian three-class electoral system. Geared as it was to agrarian economic interests, it had no current counterpart in Europe. At that time, universal and equal suffrage had just been established—very belatedly—in Great Britain. Weber considered this the only fair and modern way for a citizenry to throw off the yoke of authoritarian tutelage and participate in its government.

His opposition to electoral privileges for particular classes was conditioned chiefly by his negative attitude toward the aristocracy of the time as a social class.[4] He emphatically denied the existence of an aristocratic class in the Germany of his time and considered the aristocratic claims of the landowning Prussian Junkers an anachronistic survival of feudal times. Scathingly, he spoke of them as nothing but plebeians in their manners and opinions. Generally, in fact, Weber reserved his harshest words

---

[4] On this see especially *Pol. Schr.*, pp. 258 ff. It has occasionally been suggested that Weber, in his attitude toward aristocracy, was influenced by Friedrich Nietzsche. But for this there is no clear evidence in his writings. Aside from this it is hard to imagine two personalities more different than that of Max Weber, standing in the midst of life and affirming it, and that of Nietzsche, who lashed out against the age he despised. Max Weber regarded Nietzsche to be far more an inspired poet than a philosopher objectively analyzing reality. That was all the more true of Weber's attitude toward the poet Stefan George, whom he met on a number of occasions.

for the German way of life—in contrast to the English canon o
gentlemanliness or even the spirit of the French salon. The Wei
mar Republic also was unsuccessful in dealing with the Junkers
it took the iron broom of the East German Communists to swee
them finally from the soil of Germany.

Weber's familiarity with the authentic aristocracies of the pas
ranged from the hereditary aristocracies of Venice or Rome t
Ancient China's aristocracy of officials and scholars. He was wel
aware of the great contributions that the aristocracies had mad
to human civilization. Nevertheless, he was persuaded that b
this time aristocracy had outlived its usefulness as a politicall
creative social class. He felt that it had no future, either as
newly recreated class or as a residue of the past. This view wa
fully confirmed by subsequent history. Nowhere in the worl
has a genuine aristocracy survived or a new one been created
Even in England, inflation and the inheritance tax (the latte
introduced, by the way, by the Conservatives) have wiped ou
all but a fraction of the former landed aristocracy that used t
perform services for Great Britain similar to those the senatoria
nobility rendered to the Roman Republic. Once it had lost it
economic independence as a leisure class, which formerly pre
destined it for politics as a profession, the aristocracy had to sur
render its leadership role in government.[5]

Universal and equal suffrage, then, seemed to Weber alon
acceptable and appropriate to the needs of the day. Genuin
parliamentarization could only grow out of genuine democratiza
tion. Here again Max Weber hit the prophetic nail on the head
Since his day, universal suffrage has triumphed all over th
world. Relapses into an electoral system favoring the privileged
classes have been conspicuous by their absence. No developing

---

[5] In the United States, too, the leisure class described by Max Weber'
contemporary, Thorstein Veblen, has ceased to play a part in politics
This statement is not invalidated by the fact that certain presidentia
candidates have recently been recruited from among millionaires.

ountry, no matter how backward, can do without universal uffrage if it wishes to aspire to democratic respectability. Even he barefaced military dictatorships of our time cloak their akedness with the pseudo-legitimation of manipulated and razenly bogus general elections. Weber also correctly foresaw he part that would be played by universal suffrage in the transormation of mass democracy into Caesarism.

As far as the technical features of universal suffrage are conerned, Max Weber believed that proportional representation ould not serve as a vehicle for true political leadership[6] because, ike the plebiscitary leadership of the political parties, it was ound to lead to a "drying of the life blood of the body olitic," and to "intellectual proletarization of the party folowers." Weber regarded proportional representation a typical roduct of a "leaderless" democracy. It inevitably results, he naintained, in horse-trading among the party dignitaries to deermine who should be placed on the list, and in what rank. Worse still, representatives of interest and pressure groups are lrawn into politics whose sole concern with public life is with what their backers can get out of it. The presence of such selfish nterests depoliticizes the parliament and prevents the rise of any eal corps of leaders. When we consider that at the time—in 919—proportional representation had hardly been tested in ny mass democracy, so that the vast amount of unfavorable vidence that has since been amassed was then lacking, we must gain pay tribute to Max Weber's foresight. For proportional epresentation has since proved its value only in countries that re on the fringes of world politics, such as Switzerland, Scandiavia, the Netherlands, and Belgium—all countries which, moreover, are blessed by a politically mature population that agrees n fundamentals. In some larger and more important countries, it lourished only briefly after the First World War, quite often

---

[6] On proportional representation see *Pol. Schr.,* pp. 487 f., 531 ff.

wreaking havoc on political cohesiveness. It has never become
established in Anglo-Saxon countries; in other countries, such as
France, it has been attempted and then abandoned in favor of
the technique of majority representation. In the German Fed
eral Republic after 1945, the intention was to overcome some of
the failures of proportional representation by linking it to the
"personality election" of individual candidates. That idea
stemmed from the British Occupation authorities and was in it
self a happy variant. But the Germans only jumped from the fry
ing pan into the fire when they tried to achieve governmental
stability—always imperiled by a multi-party system—by intro
ducing the nefarious "five per cent clause," under which a party
is permitted to participate in the distribution of the votes cast
for the common pool only if it has obtained at least five per
cent of the total electoral vote. That clause is completely un
democratic in character, despite the fact that the highest federal
courts in Germany (and in Switzerland) have declared it con
stitutional, for it is simply an indirect gift to the existing political
parties. Fundamentally, it has no more justification than the out
right gift of additional seats to the strongest party that has been
tried at times in Republican Italy, in imitation of Mussolini's
practices. Max Weber's indictment of proportional representa
tion has thus today become an axiom of political science.[7]

3. *The Position of the Bureaucracy in Modern Society*

If Max Weber identified any single factor as Political Enemy
Number 1, it was the untrammeled rule of a bureaucracy. What
he meant by the bureaucracy was the scientifically trained staff,
hierarchically organized and equipped with special technological
knowledge, which is entrusted with the administration of the
state. His study of history convinced him that an entrenched

---

[7] On Max Weber's rejection of the vocational franchise, see above pp
26 f.

bureaucracy never reforms itself of its own accord, and it vanishes only when the state it controls has been obliterated. In universal terms, bureaucratic control is the fate of any and all societies. No organized state can subsist without such a bureaucracy. What makes modern bureaucracy inescapable is its specialization and efficient technical training.[8] The real dilemma arises when those who hold political responsibility let the leadership slip from their hands and into the possession of the anonymous and therefore irresponsible bureaucracy.[9] In Wilhelminian Germany, Max Weber had ample opportunity to observe how bureaucrats, conscious of and obsessed with power, arrogated to themselves the function of political decision-making and used it for their own ends. He did not accept the argument, popular at the time, that a responsible bureaucracy would meet the needs of the people of its own volition. A state dominated by certificated officials would fall prey to a kind of Chinese mandarinism and lead to utter stagnation, he maintained. Parliamentarism seemed to him the only possible protection against bureaucratic domination. Only genuine parliamentarism, which would create a body of responsible political leaders, could successfully countervail the omnipotence of bureaucracy.

In this fundamental thesis of Max Weber's political sociology we have a correct premise and an incorrect conclusion. The past half-century has completely confirmed his belief that the mass state society is condemned to bureaucracy. On the other hand, it seems dubious that parliamentarism can offset the domination of such a bureaucracy. The legislative state of his time, which was directed primarily by the parliament, has been transformed into the present-day administrative state, which by necessity must be managed by the bureaucracy. By the same token, the individual's demands upon his government have risen to an inconceivable

---

[8] *Pol. Schr.*, p. 317.
[9] *Pol. Schr.*, p. 278.

degree. And as the administrative has more and more evolved into the welfare state—and where is that not happening today? —bureaucratic administration has swelled and proliferated. We need only think of the ever-increasing social services that the citizen claims as his right—and which inevitably bring him into daily contact with the bureaucracy. Such expansion requires an inexorably growing army of administrative specialists who distribute these social services. The well-known and incontrovertible formula of "Parkinson's Law" postulates that such a bureaucratic apparatus is, by its very nature, always increasing.

But the matter does not end there. We must remember that the concept of bureaucracy includes not only actual state officials but functionaries in general. All other social organizations outside the state have likewise become bureaucratized. This is especially valid for all political parties. No longer controlled by the leisure class—as they were in the days of limited suffrage—they have transformed themselves into gigantic business enterprises efficiently administered by a professional party bureaucracy. That holds not only for the totalitarian parties, whose structure is fully bureaucratic and hierarchical, but for all bourgeois and especially all socialist parties, which, dependent on enlisting the support of the masses, have become bureaucratic organizations. They had no choice but to become so, if they were to find means for efficiently raising campaign funds.[10] The iron law of bureaucratization applies, however, first and foremost to all professional associations and interest groups in our infinitely multifarious pluralistic society. Pluralism and bureaucracy are sisters emerging from the same womb. Every individual is entangled in a network of pluralistic dependency relationships. He is a unit of the collective that paternalistically controls and directs him, and in its turn is run by its functionaries.

But having engulfed this much, the insatiable leviathan of

---

[10] *Pol. Schr.*, p. 316.

bureaucracy is not yet satisfied. Capitalistic business concerns, to the extent that they have outgrown small business or family firms (and the tendency everywhere is toward big business organized in anonymous corporations or stock companies), are directed by a specially trained managerial class of functionaries, which, with its regular promotions and pensions, is heavily bureaucratized. Business firms frequently assume the task of training their own replacement personnel. The phenomenon of the organization man, devoted body and soul to his company, was first observed in America, but is spreading throughout the capitalist world. In certain environments, as in modern Japan, the system assumes the forms of a new economic feudalism, in which the company is the lord, the employees are the vassals and retainers. The entrepreneurs, for their part, are organized in associations, cartels, and trusts. They are likewise directed by a specialized bureaucracy whose services resemble those of government officials. Among them, the capitalistic profit motive recedes; what comes to the fore is economic security guaranteed by fixed employment. Among employees, bureaucratization of the unions and the white-collar associations is just as pronounced. Thus Weber's prediction of the irresistible growth of bureaucracy has proved true in all spheres of human activity.

Finally, Max Weber's prognosis of what would follow should private capitalism some day be eliminated now appears uncannily prophetic. "A breakdown of the steel casing of the industrial structure? . . . No. Rather the management of the nationalized industries, or those organized into some kind of 'association' would become bureaucratic. . . . If private capitalism were done away with, the state bureaucracy alone would dominate." Furthermore, Weber drew the picture of that "future state of universal subservience when all of mankind may be reduced to the helpless obedience of the fellahin in ancient Egypt . . . when the bureaucratic administration . . . itself will decide how its affairs are to be directed."[11] No one who reads these lines today can fail to recognize the terrifying lineaments of the totalitarian state.

In retrospect, we are bound to realize Weber's error in expecting that parliamentarization would limit the domination of the bureaucracy and bring it under the control of the political leadership. We must, however, refrain from any general verdict because developments in different countries have proceeded along different lines.

In Germany, at any rate, the hoped-for effect has not taken place. German parliamentarism, from which an elite leadership should have risen organically, experienced extraordinary difficulties in getting started: the Damoclean sword of reparations, the disastrous inflation, and the hardly less catastrophic deflation. Wherever any leadership showed signs of developing, it was crushed by fratricidal parliamentary strife.

But even without such problems, Weimar would not have been able to strip the bureaucracy of its power. The fox was set to mind the sheep in Weimar. That is, unlike most western and above all Anglo-Saxon countries, civil servants were permitted to hold parliamentary mandates. In fact, they were actually encouraged to run for elective office, on the ground that they alone possessed the technical knowledge indispensable for legislation.

Napoleon had been able to make use of the bureaucratic centralism he inherited from the *ancien régime* because the Revolution had destroyed the old class of civil servants, and he had created an imperial bureaucracy of his own to replace them. The new officialdom, far from dominating him, was in his hand a pliable instrument of governing. In the young Weimar Republic, on the other hand, any political purge would be blocked by cries of "vested rights." The result was that the same personnel remained at the helm as before 1918. Supposedly, they accepted

---

[11] The quotations above (condensed here) will be found in *Pol. Schr.*, pp. 319 f.

"the facts of republicanism"; in practice they sailed under monarchistic and anti-democratic flags and did their utmost to scuttle the Republic. The weak parliamentary leaders failed to defend themselves against these officials. Moreover, during the last years of the Weimar Republic, the parliament was so divided by partisanship that the ministerial bureaucracy could do exactly as it pleased. By virtue of the emergency ordinances it imposed on the basis of Article 48 of the Constitution, it acted as actual legislator, impervious to any control. Thus the Weimar Republic was politically and administratively no less dominated by the bureaucracy than the Empire had been.

The result was that German officialdom offered not the slightest resistance to Hitler's despotism. The bureaucrats were concerned only with saving their professional skins, even though it meant giving up all their political influence to the Nazi Party bureaucracy, which was anything but trained for its tasks. The collapse of 1945 might have provided one of those rare opportunities for a housecleaning and renovation of officialdom. But in spite of some well-meaning though amateurish efforts on the part of the Occupation authorities, the chance was thrown away. No sooner had the Occupying Powers relaxed their pressure, when a solid phalanx of officials insisted on having the totality of their former power restored to them (as evidenced by the controversy over Article 131 of the Constitution). As a result, today the professional class of officials, chiefly represented by the ministerial bureaucracy in the federal government and the states, has once again become an unassailable pillar of the Bonn regime. Nor has anything been done about that most baneful feature of German parliamentarism: the habit of public officials of taking furloughs from their government jobs to serve as members of the parliaments of the cabinets. In spite of elaborate deals to distribute ministerial positions among the parties, the leading posts in the ministerial bureaucracy are assigned in accordance with the goals of the majority party. Hence the bureaucratization of politics in both the federal government and the states appears unalterable, in Germany at least—contrary to Max Weber's hopes. In Scandinavia, the device of parliamentary commissioner *(Ombudsman)* has been tried as a check on the bureaucracy. It has now been introduced into New Zealand, and is being considered in other western countries (England, Australia, Switzerland, Canada, and also in a few American states). Its effectiveness as a counterweight to the bureaucracy cannot as yet be conclusively judged; but recent experiences in Germany with a parliamentary commissioner for matters of defense has scarcely been encouraging.

Outside of Germany the situation, when viewed retrospectively, is less uniform. In France the bureaucracy has been the power behind the political scenes ever since the *ancien régime.* At times during the Third and Fourth Republics, it had to share its monopoly with the parliamentary leadership; but the chronic instability of the cabinets played into its hands, since it was, in a constantly fluid situation, the only stable center. Under de Gaulle its principal representatives, the young "technocrats," completely dominate the national stage. They have had no rivals because the policy of de-emphasizing parliament has, for the time being, completely paralyzed the former parliamentary leadership. The high quality of the French corps of professional officials, which was energetically modernized and democratized by the much maligned Fourth Republic, makes this development less sinister—but does not alter the fundamental fact that the bureaucracy is completely in the saddle.

Things are still otherwise in the Anglo-Saxon countries, with differences between Great Britain and the United States. In England too the irresistible advance of the administrative state has given rise to complaints about the "new despotism" of the bureaucracy (Lord Hewart of Burley and others); but unlike the Continent, there has been some thinning of the trees in the bureaucratic forests. Parliamentary control over the administration, which was what Max Weber obviously had in mind, on the whole has been effective in England. That is apparent to anyone who has ever attended a question period in the House of Commons—even though the members must understandably content themselves with random sampling. Above all (and this is the decisive factor), the British civil servant by tradition and professional ethics practices the strictest political neutrality. He serves every government, no matter what its party complexion, with the same professional zeal, and has neither desire nor ambition to influence political decisions.[12] Yet it must be said that true parliamentary control of the administration, in spite of all the requirements to submit administrative regulations to Parliament, is largely nominal in England, just as it is elsewhere. In the first place, Parliament actually has no time to make thorough investigations; in the second place, M.P.'s lack the requisite technical knowledge. And in the nationalized industries and social services, in all those aspects of economic and social life that belong to the public sector, the officials in charge have quickly taken over the reins. Parliamentary supervision has almost totally failed in this realm. This does not mean that an uncontrollable bureaucracy will curtail the liberties of the citizenry; for like the Civil Service proper, the administrative bureaucracy in such state-owned branches of the economy and welfare services has no political ambitions and is concerned solely with effectively carrying out its tasks.

As for bureaucracy in the United States—even in Max Weber's day it was undergoing a transformation that apparently

---

[12] The following sentences from "Parlament und Regierung im neugeordneten Deutschland" (*Pol. Schr.*, pp. 339 f.), while not referring to England in their context, may serve as an accurate description of the British official: "[the professional official] takes pride in preserving impartiality and being able to overcome his own inclinations and opinions in order to carry out conscientiously and skilfully whatever general regulations or special instructions require of him, even—and in fact especially—when they do *not* correspond to his own political views."

escaped him. He treated the American public service as still subject to the spoils system, as it had been during the nineteenth
century and still was to some extent at the time of his visit to the
United States.[13] But even then the spoils system had largely given
way to the present permanent civil service based on competitive
examinations. Today this professional officialdom is in charge,
except for a few thousand so-called policy-making posts at the
disposal of the party in power.[14] The completely depoliticized
officialdom in the United States today forms neither a class nor
a state within the state, nor does it have political ambitions. The
civil service is exclusively an administrative instrument of the executive branch. Due to the still current set of social values in
America, it is held in far less respect than is the official class in
continental Europe or in Great Britain. In the matter on which
Max Weber laid such stress—parliamentary control of officialdom—Congress has proved as powerless as have its European
counterparts. On the one hand, this is due to the separation of
powers in the United States; on the other, the federal administrative apparatus has become so huge and complicated that Congress cannot possibly attempt to supervise it.

In addition, in contrast to the strict departmental or ministerial
structure of the administration in Europe, America operates the
so-called Independent Regulatory Agencies.[15] To these are entrusted the most important administrative areas, especially what
is wildly misnamed government control of business. Partly because of Congressional intention when they were set up, partly
because of an inescapable evolutionary process, they have become

---

[13] See *Pol. Schr.*, pp. 457, 497, 526, 529.

[14] See Karl Loewenstein, *Verfassungrecht und Verfassungspraxis der
Vereinigten Staaten* (Berlin, Göttingen, Heidelberg: Springer, 1959) (=
Enzyklopädie der Rechts- und Staatswissenschaft, Abt. Rechtswissen-
schaft), pp. 356 ff.

[15] See *op. cit.,* pp. 356 ff. and the author's special study: "Die Krise
des amerikanischen Rundfunk- und Fernsehwesen," in *Archiv des öffent-
lichen Rechts.,* vol. 86 (1961), pp. 404 ff.

"independent" of the President and of the departments subordinate to him and also independent of Congress itself. The result, which has recently given rise to much complaint, is that the agencies that are supposed to regulate industries tend to become the captives of these very industries. Thus we may conclude that in the United States as well, parliamentary control of the bureaucracy has not succeeded; yet the failure has had no political consequences because the bureaucracy has no influence and no desire to exert it.

Now, however, we shall have to ask ourselves whether Max Weber, from his Germanocentric viewpoint, did not overestimate the dangers of uncontrolled bureaucracy, or at any rate the danger that it might impose non-statutory or arbitrary restrictions upon the life of the individual citizen. Nowhere in his writings on the subject do we find any discussion on the institution of independent administrative courts as possible recourse against administrative abuses and arbitrariness.[16] Granted, judicial control of the administration was underdeveloped in imperial Germany; such control was only instituted under the Weimar Republic, with its deeper concern for civil rights. Since Weber's time the courts have developed into a genuine Third Power throughout the western constitutional democracies. On the whole, then, the lance that Max Weber hurled against bureaucratic omnipotence missed its mark. The parliaments have proved unequal to the task of curbing bureaucracy, but the courts have stepped into the breach. Even in Max Weber's time that was certainly true for France, where ever since the eighteen-seventies the Conseil d'État shouldered the task of protecting the citizen from administrative abuses. The ordinary French citizen thus has a recourse against *excès de pouvoir* and *détournement*

---

16 Not even in the *Rechtssoziologie,* which would have been the proper place for it; the work contains only a single and unimportant reference to administrative jurisdiction (edition: Neuwied, Luchterhand, 1960 [= *Soziologische Texte,* vol. 2], p. 91).

de pouvoir. In England, likewise, a number of special administrative tribunals, different from the ordinary courts, have been established for the same purposes. In the United States, where there seems to be less need for such protection, the regular courts can always intervene. Weimar, and especially Bonn, furthered the system of independent judicial review of administrative acts. In addition, truly independent courts for constitutional questions have been created to deal with any infringement of the rule of law by the highest organs of the government. We may say, then, that today Max Weber's demands for the end of administrative secrecy and impartial control of the administrative services have been largely met.

4. *Parliamentarism as the Generating Force for Political Leadership*

At the end of the First World War, Max Weber was still deeply concerned with Germany's future form of government—monarchy or (parliamentary) republic. He was guided by the classical tenets of the general theory of the state as elaborated by Roscher, Bluntschli, Treitschke, and Jellinek. Under pressure of circumstances he finally decided in favor of a parliamentary republic, although he was well aware that it would be handicapped by the burden of defeat.[17] Today, the form of government means little to us and the pattern of government a great deal—since that determines the way in which the state organs must cooperate to arrive at political decisions. Max Weber, too, really placed his stress on what pattern of government was to be chosen. On the basis of his comparative typology of law, he clearly perceived that—in the words we have already quoted: "In the simple questions of the technique of arriving at policy decisions, the mass state does not permit unlimited choice. There are only a re-

---

[17] *Pol. Schr.,* pp. 437 ff.

stricted number of forms."[18] Since neither the American presidential nor the Swiss directory type of government was suitable for Germany, the only remaining alternative was the parliamentary republic.[19] If there were any doubts as to what this term meant, his frequent references to the example of England should have made the connotations clear. He described the dynamics of parliamentary government in England as follows:[20] The administrative heads (ministers) must either be drawn from the parliament *(parliamentary system in the proper sense)* or, at any rate, be dependent upon a vote of confidence by parliament in order to stay in office *(parliamentary selection of leaders)*. They must be subject to questioning by parliament or its committees *(parliamentary responsibility of the leaders)* and direct the administration along the guidelines approved by parliament *(parliamentary administrative control)*. Weber's definition of the political leader fits these conditions: "A political leader is not someone who seeks office for the sake of its salary and pension. Neither is he bent on exercising some bureaucratic function with the minimum of outside control. What he seeks is political power—which means politically responsible power based on the confidence and adherence of a party. As a minister, he will want to remain at the head or in the midst of that party, if only to maintain his influence over it."[21]

Measured against this English "ideal type," have Weber's hopes of a parliamentary government for Germany been fulfilled? There is no question that he considered it was feasible, in

---

[18] *Pol. Schr.*, p. 295.

[19] The statement at the beginning of the newspaper article "Innere Lage und Aussenpolitik" (*Pol. Schr.*, pp. 280 ff.), written in February 1919, that Bolshevism would last for only a few months, was of course a monumental misjudgment. But compare the far more perspicacious comments in "Politik als Beruf," written more than a year later (*Pol. Schr.*, p. 517).

[20] See *Pol. Schr.*, p. 328.

[21] *Pol. Schr.*, p. 412.

spite of Germany's tradition of subservience to authority. He inveighed against the "idle talk of an incompatibility between the 'West European' and the 'German' concept of government"[22] —talk which to this day, after half a century, recurs in the covert, but fairly common assertion that the Germans are "not ripe" for democracy. But almost in the same breath, Weber's profound skepticism breaks through: "Whether a really workable parliamentary system will come into Germany, we do not know. It might equally well be undermined by the Right or foolishly thrown overboard by the Left."[23] Truly prophetic words!

What, then, did he expect of German parliamentarism under the most auspicious conditions? From his discussion of the ingredients of classical English parliamentarism, we see that he thought of the parliamentary process as the most desirable means, not only for controlling bureaucracy, but also for the creation of leadership. He would probably be intensely disappointed by what has actually taken place, although as an historian he was aware that the man of politics "must think in terms of generations, when considering problems of statecraft."[24]

In extenuation of the Weimar Republic, it must be said that it was born and lived under an unlucky star. It was not given time, in terms of generations, in which to wrestle with its problems. Weimar simply had no chance to develop an organic procedure for the parliamentary creation of political leadership. Only a few years of pseudo-prosperity could be interpolated between the aftermath of the war, with its inflation, and the economic crisis caused by the world-wide depression. The Republic was also sorely pressed by the reparation demands of the Allies, who still believed that the cost of the war must be borne by the vanquished.

Nevertheless, the Weimar system, as such, had faults which

---

[22] *Pol. Schr.*, p. 296.
[23] *Pol. Schr.*, p. 297.
[24] *Pol. Schr.*, p. 298.

should not be minimized. The fundamental defect has been mentioned: the practice of drawing cabinet ministers from officials or from among non-political experts outside the parliament. Bureaucrats on leave, they were rank outsiders who could not generate a parliamentary *esprit de corps*. Consequently, they were the poorest sort of material for a political leadership. Max Weber had been thinking of a parliament that would wield power. But the Weimar parliament was hamstrung by the notorious Article 48 of the Constitution, which released the administration from any responsibility to parliament. The Third French Republic in its declining days suffered similar debilitation from the abuse of the *pleins pouvoirs*. But even when prominent party leaders from outside officialdom took over some cabinet posts, the multiparty system bred by proportional representation prevented the rise of a genuine elite leadership. For in the inevitable coalition government, cabinet posts were assigned by horse-trading. Thus nine-day-wonders in party politics became government ministers—men who did not remotely qualify for membership in that standing group of top-flight candidates who are called *ministrables* on the Continent. Excessive attrition of potential cabinet members prevented the formation of an organic leadership, let alone an elite corps of real leaders.

In Bonn the multiparty system has been much reduced, although it has not entirely vanished; at the present time there are still four distinct parties in the federal parliament. Nevertheless, the ways for developing parliamentary leadership have not been essentially improved under the Bonn regime. That is all the more regrettable because Bonn functions under much more favorable conditions than did the Weimar Republic. Instead of being subject to continual pressure from former enemy powers, the Federal Republic has risen rapidly to the position of a courted ally of the victors. Nevertheless, things have not taken the happiest turn in Bonn, where Adenauer's fourteen years of authoritarian rule once again discouraged the rise of a group of responsible leaders. A good deal of the blame must also be ascribed to the "chancellor principle," laid down in the Constitution: since the federal chancellor alone is responsible to parliament, the cabinet ministers are downgraded to mere tools of the chancellor.

Had Adenauer not insisted on overshadowing all rivals, it would have been possible and useful for the Christian Democratic Union, as long as it remained the permanent government party, to build up a group of leaders within its ranks. But as a rule, only a few cabinet ministers succeeded in holding their posts after new elections, and these ministers could scarcely be considered members of an "elite."* As the Bonn system has worked out so far, it may, with some justification, be labeled "demo-authoritarian." The chancellor comes to power by genuine democratic techniques, which are plebiscitary as well as representative. But his rule is authoritarian during the period between elections. The Bundestag cannot remove him because of the "constructive" vote of no-confidence.† Hence, the chancellor can haughtily ignore any rising tide of popular opposition.

What is more, the Bonn political climate has so far been hostile to the emergence of an elite leadership. Nor has there been any provision for the development of such leadership in the party that potentially may replace the government party in power. Bonn has nothing like the well-known English institution of a "shadow cabinet." Leadership in Bonn has therefore fallen

---

* This pattern was broken after the elections of 1965, when practically all the members of Chancellor Erhard's Cabinets remained in office, though in a number of cases, their posts were shuffled. This fact does not invalidate the stricture in the text concerning their lack of leadership qualities.

† This refers to the provision in Article 67 of the Bonn Constitution which stipulates that the chancellor can be removed from office by a vote of no confidence only when the federal parliament simultaneously agrees by majority vote on his successor, who is then to be installed in office by the federal president.

willy-nilly to the top officials of the ministerial bureaucracy—a state of affairs Weber would have gravely deplored. In fairness, however, it must be said that Bonn has proved more fortunate or more adept than Weimar in selecting its personnel. Certain small beginnings justify the hope that a real leadership may in time develop. Efforts should certainly be made, however, to break once and for all with the time-honored practice of having cabinet ministers who are not members of the parliament—as was the case with the holder of the important defense ministry until 1965.

The contrast between authentic and specious parliamentarism emerges clearly from a comparison of Weimar and Bonn with Great Britain. Max Weber repeatedly stressed[25] that the British Parliament had been the model school for the training of an elite political leadership—and, we must now add, has remained so up to the present day.

No one in England can attain a cabinet position—which means the only possible access to effective political power—unless he has climbed up the parliamentary ladder. Some do it slowly, some quickly; but every potential leader is thus forced to demonstrate his political qualities to the party leadership and before the bar of public opinion. In the British political milieu, there is no room for a non-parliamentary demagogue—and none has appeared on the political stage within living memory. The English are therefore in the enviable position of always having on top a political team consisting of people who are indubitably amateurs in technical matters, but professionals in political affairs. These amateurs have the political experience and social know-how to direct their professional officials and, if need be, to keep these officials within bounds. As Weber saw it, their work

---

[25] See, e.g., *Pol. Schr.*, p. 343 and *passim*. See his remark *ibid.*, p. 343: ". . . After all this body has been the site for the selection of those statesmen who have known how to subordinate a fourth of humanity to the rule of a tiny political minority."

on committees was a particularly valuable part of their training.
He correctly recognized that universal suffrage, which had ju
(1918) been introduced, would strengthen, rather than weake
parliamentarism. He also foresaw the crumbling of the tw
party system as a result of the rise of the Labour Party,
though he could not have known that the healthy political i
stinct of the British people would shortly lead the nation back
the habitual system of two and only two alternating parties.

The much-maligned Third and Fourth French Republics we
also able to establish a genuine elite leadership of *ministrables* b
a system of parliamentary co-optation. In the course of the fr
quent cabinet crises, the ministerial candidates played music
chairs among the ministries. Though they passed from one ministr
to another, they were often in a position to place their politic
experience at the disposal of the country for decades. Men lik
Clemenceau, Briand, Poincaré, and Tardieu in the Third, an
Marie, Mollet, Pinay, and Pflimlin in the Fourth Republic, ha
qualities of leadership scarcely inferior to those of the corr
sponding English teams. The de Gaulle regime, however, ha
virtually eliminated parliament as a school of political leade
ship. De Gaulle has autocratically ordained various "changes o
the guard" in the ministries. He has deliberately cultivated
"his" parliament the "will to impotence" which Max Weber s
sharply denounced in the Bismarckian Reichstag. Such method
have seriously impaired the process of rearing an experience
parliamentary leadership. It remains to be seen whether, afte
the passing of the plebiscitary leader, the French tradition of
leadership group consisting of ministrables will reassert itself.

---

26 Max Weber probably overestimated the importance of the grea
parliamentary investigations in shedding light on administrative pra
tices. The golden age of these inquiries was the nineteenth century
Today, they have largely given way to the non-parliamentary Roya
Commissions.

27 Cf. *Pol. Schr.*, p. 371.

The problem of leadership is something else again in the non-parliamentary countries of Switzerland and the United States. In the Swiss Confederation, the acknowledged leadership group, the members of the Federal Council, are first filtered through the sieve of parliament and the party directorates. Thus non-entities are excluded. In the United States, on the other hand, a leading elite cannot form within the government itself because each president picks a new cabinet, preferably from his own party. The cabinet members are usually politicians or businessmen who often return to their main occupation before the end of an administration. It is rare for them to be called into office again. On the other hand, various circumstances help to produce in Congress a considerable corps of prominent veterans. Concerned with re-election, they are reluctant to accept positions in the administration, preferring instead long-term membership on committees. These men, however, hardly qualify for the term of elite leadership.

Once more, looking backward, we realize that in the last half-century the power of the executive branch of government has steadily increased at the expense of the power of parliaments. This holds for executive power embodied in a prime minister or in the collective leadership cabinet. Wherever parliamentarism has survived in the Western world, the parliament itself has yielded to the pressure of the irresistibly advancing executive branch. The parliaments have been so weakened that they can no longer adequately perform their primary task of acting as a check on the government. Even in England, the situation is such that the government of the party that has come to power in the general elections can no longer be deposed. Iron party discipline keeps the British Cabinet in power, even as the chancellor in the German Federal Republic is sustained in power by the "constructive" vote of no-confidence. In countries governed by multiparty coalitions, the fear of dissolution keeps the parliaments from intervening in the work of the administration. Thus the characteristic political feature of our time is a strong executive endowed with true political leadership. Plebiscitary elections and the oligarchic nature of the policy-making function (which Max Weber was completely aware of) have produced this strong executive. Again, we must accede to Weber's insight that the value of the parliament does not lie in the institution as such, but chiefly in its capacity to produce political leadership, which, in mass democracies, may be pitted against the plebiscitary leader.

To sum up: in states with parliamentary "rule"—as they are mislabeled—the government has long since outrun parliament. The United States, where Congress remains in a very strong position, must be left out of consideration, since it does not conform to the pattern of classical parliamentarism. Where we have neo-presidentialism after the manner of de Gaulle, parliamentary impotence is written into the very constitution, and the parliament scarcely can operate effectively against the strong chief of state. And wherever the new countries have set up a parliament, their one-party systems have made it only a shadow cast by the all-powerful president. All the world over, constitutional democracy has been forced on the defensive. All these matters combined help to explain why parliamentarism, which in the nineteenth century seemed to be the ultimate in political wisdom, has today undergone such widespread devaluation. Parliaments no longer serve as the foci of power.

5. The Position of the Second Chamber in the Parliamentary System

In Germany the upper chamber of parliament (the Reichsrat and Bundesrat respectively) by established tradition is regarded primarily as an organ of the states, with an important part to play in federal administration. Consequently, it is not constituted, as in most western countries, as a genuine upper house which participates in legislative functions alongside the popularly elected house of representatives. This feature seems to be a peculiarity of German political thought that goes back to Bismarck and probably even further. Max Weber fully understood the fundamental distinction between a system of delegates and one of representatives, as is clear from comparisons he draws with the American Senate and the Swiss Council of States. Nevertheless, Weber finally bowed to German tradition and accepted the federalistic functions of the upper house.[28] He took occasion, however, to analyze carefully the position of the upper house within the structure of a parliamentary state. Once again his views were shaped by the example of England. There, barely a decade earlier, the House of Lords had opposed—for selfish reasons of economic interest—the manifest will of the popularly elected lower house. It had taken a grave constitutional crisis to abridge the power of the upper house.

In a period of spreading democratization, Weber argued, an upper house can be formally "only a chamber with lesser powers whose limited though important task is in being an advisory, criticizing body, able to delay legislation by suspensive veto but unable to permanently block the desires of an indisputably strong majority of the popular representatives on a politically important question."[29] The upper house is necessarily subordinate to the lower, if only because it lacks budgetary powers. The virtue of a chamber based on popular election but representing the states, on the other hand, is the smaller membership. This gives it "intensified ability to act and make more precise, strictly rational decisions determined less by emotionality and demagoguery."[30] In advancing these arguments, Max Weber was far ahead of his times; for the upper houses in many countries, especially in Germany, were then citadels of class privilege. What he says about

---

[28] See *Pol. Schr.*, pp. 452 ff. and above, pp. 18 ff.
[29] *Pol. Schr.*, pp. 247 ff.
[30] *Pol. Schr.*, pp. 452 f.

the usefulness of an upper house with reasonably circumscribed functions reads like a description of the present House of Lords: "A center for individual political eloquence, for the expression of diverse political opinion and the employment of political intelligence by men holding no office, but experienced in office, embodying a group of former statesmen with their extensive experience as contrasted to the present leadership of the political parties."[31] To be sure, these words apply only to the notoriously small group of peers who actively participate in the work of the House of Lords.

Once again Weber made an accurate prediction of the political future of the upper houses in parliamentary states. For after the virtual decapitation of the House of Lords by the Parliament Acts of 1911 (and 1949), the upper houses have almost everywhere been reduced to playing second fiddle to the lower houses. The fate of the French Senate under the Third and Fourth Republics, let alone the Fifth, makes that plain. Italy under the constitution of 1947 is an exception. The predominant position of the Senate in the (non-parliamentary) United States derives from the broader powers assigned to it from the start by the Constitution. But even in America the relationship of the two chambers has somewhat fallen into line with the world-wide trend. The House of Representatives has managed to obtain some hold over foreign policy, formerly the Senate's monopoly, by its powers to appropriate money. Another significant sign of the decline of the two-chamber system is New Zealand's abandonment of it. Though more British than the British, the New Zealanders have dropped the British model in this respect and gone over to a single-chamber system. Moreover, a number of the most modern constitutions—those of Greece, Denmark, Israel, and virtually all the former colonial countries that have achieved sovereignty (except Madagascar) have been converted to the

[31] *Pol. Schr.*, p. 248.

one-chamber system and have entirely dispensed with a second chamber sharing the political power. The recent establishment of the two-chamber system in Turkey is due to political rather than organizational reasons; the military men who dominate the government fear the political parties that represent the popular will.

We need only mention briefly that Max Weber sharply rejected the ideas of suffrage based on occupational groups and of a second chamber to represent such groups. His arguments remain the classic statement of the case.[32] It would be completely impossible, he maintained, to divide the electorate into economic groups and to organize a parliament according to their economic interests. The infinite complexity of constantly fluctuating economic life cannot be reduced to mechanical formulas. "In an age of constant technical and commercial reshufflings and continuous realignment of economic and social affiliations, it is the height of impractical absurdity to attempt the creation of political electorates as 'organic' associations in the old sense of the estates."[33]

Experience with so-called "economic parliaments" has since borne out Max Weber's skepticism. The *Reichswirtschaftsrat* (Federal Economic Council) of the Weimar Republic (Art. 165) was stillborn. Similar experiments by the Third and Fourth Republics were pitched on a more modest key and therefore proved more successful. The Economic Council was able to offer useful advice to economic planners, but did not presume a claim to share in political decisions. Max Weber's scathing denunciation of occupational representation might well be read with profit by those romantic muddleheads in present-day Germany who imagine that a return to the good old days of feudal "estates of the realm" would provide a way out of wicked modern party-dominated parliamentarism.

---

[32] *Pol. Schr.*, pp. 313 f.
[33] *Pol. Schr.*, p. 244.

6. *The Techniques of Direct Democracy*

In his political writings, Weber devotes a surprising amount of attention to direct democracy—initiative, referendum, and recall —in a parliamentary democracy.[34]

The French Revolution might be regarded as the arena for the intellectual and practical confrontation between Montesquieu and Rousseau. Montesquieu considered representative government the only possible constitutional arrangement for political decision-making. Rousseau, with his mystical faith that the "general will" was embodied in the people, rejected the techniques of representation and demanded direct expression of the desires of the citizenry.[35] The actual organization of nineteenth-century states was based on the views of Edmund Burke and Abbé Sieyès, that is, representation in the form of a parliament legitimized by popular election. But direct manifestation of the people's will has since repeatedly come to the fore, chiefly in plebiscites to decide questions of sovereignty (territorial changes or the form of government). In Max Weber's time institutions of direct democracy were to be found only in Switzerland—in the federal government, the cantons, and communities—and in a number of the newer American states. Weber may have become acquainted with these institutions during his stay in the United States. The general theory of government in Max Weber's time paid relatively little attention to direct democracy. Nevertheless, with the authoritarian state breaking up, such problems were in the air, and Max Weber was right to consider them—even though he was quite aware that the new political order in Germany would necessarily diverge sharply from that of Switzerland, the indigenous habitat of direct democracy, where conditions were simpler and less sophisticated.

---

[34] *Pol. Schr.*, pp. 277 ff., 382 ff., 462 ff.

[35] See, for detailed discussion, Karl Loewenstein, *Volk und Parlament nach der Staatsauffassung der französischen Nationalversammlung von*

The referendum commended itself as an unequivocal manifestation of the people's sovereign will. Thus it would have a high educational value for a people unaccustomed to participation in politics. Moreover, it can also serve as a useful corrective; it enables the electorate to keep a check on the party-dominated parliament. But Weber also cautioned against overestimating its importance and regarding it as a universal panacea. The technique of referendum has inherent limits because the people can answer complex questions only with a yes or no vote. Hence it may prevent the possible and desirable balancing out of interests and party attitudes that can take place in parliamentary decisions. Experience in Switzerland and America has since confirmed Weber's additional warning that the referendum does not infallibly serve the cause of progress. On the contrary, it tends to be a conservating and progress-retarding force.[36] The educational value of the referendum also appears to depend much on the milieu where it is practiced. Excessive use leads, as Swiss practice has shown, to blunting rather than stimulating popular interest in politics. On the other hand, as the example of Switzerland has likewise proved, the electorate tends to ignore party guidance and positions on the subject of the referendum.

Given all these problems, what usefulness would the referendum have for Germany?[37] Max Weber regarded it as the proper *ultima ratio,* chiefly for constitutional changes and for cases of outright conflict between the highest organs in the government—or what the Constitution of the present Federal Republic calls the "supreme federal organs," which come under the jurisdiction of the Federal Constitutional Court. Weber wished to reserve the initiative for proposals backed by very large numbers

---

1789 (Münich: Drei Masken Verlag, 1922; reprinted Aalen, Würtemberg: Scientia, 1964).

[36] *Pol. Schr.,* pp. 462 f.

[37] *Pol. Schr.,* p. 388.

of citizens—he suggested one-fifth of the voters.[38] His recom
mendations were reflected in the Constitution of the Weima
Republic (Arts. 72 ff.). In his time, it could not be foreseer
that practical application of direct democracy in the milieu of
Weimar would produce nothing but misfirings. In the light o.
these failures, the drafters of the Bonn Constitution dispensed
with the institution altogether, except for the special case of ter
ritorial changes. This led to the accusation, not entirely un
justified, of anti-popular bias and overemphasis on representa
tive techniques. Nevertheless, the Federal Constitutional Court
did not see fit to alter the situation, although it had the opportunity.

On the other hand, the fresh tide of democracy that swept is
after the Second World War has once more brought the popular
referendum into fashion. It is still employed for acts of sovereignty, such as the transition from monarchy to republic (Italy)
or union with a neighboring state (Cameroons in Africa). But
in most new constitutions it is also prescribed for the adoption
of the constitution itself, and occasionally for amendments to
the constitution. In many cases the means by which the electorate
decides constitutional questions have imperceptively slid over
into the plebiscite, which modern constitutional theory rightly
distinguished from purely legislative referenda.[39] Plebiscites—
manipulated—on constitutions imposed from above, or on the
installation of a dictator as president or chief of state have be
come indispensable to the repertory of authoritarian states. They
are equally essential to the management of neo-presidential governments. The de Gaulle regime has so far held no fewer than
four referenda. Two of these concerned constitutional questions
as such, but two—in connection with the Algerian problem—
were presented as genuine plebiscites on policy decisions.

---

[38] *Pol. Schr.*, p. 463.
[39] See Karl Loewenstein, *Political Power* . . . ,   pp. 271 ff.

Why have the techniques of direct democracy undergone so surprising a revival? The reasons are not to be found in any belief in the greater political maturity of the people. In any case, there is no scientific evidence for such a belief, methods of direct democracy having also become commonplace in primitive countries that have just emerged from colonialism. Rather, the reasons must be sought in the Machiavellian attitudes of rulers who feel that government control over the mass media permits manipulation of the popular vote more easily than management of even the most effectively muzzled parliament which operates publicly. Another reason for the contemporary ubiquitousness of the plebiscite is its pseudo-democratic legitimacy. The manifest assent of the people is supposed to testify, in the eyes of the world, to a despotic regime's respectability. Hitler held plebiscites on the merger of the chancellorship with the presidency in his person and on the annexation of Austria by the Third Reich. Whether he believed in the genuineness of these popular votes cannot be determined; certainly Goebbels did not believe in them. The case of de Gaulle no doubt differs. His mystical vein is probably strong enough so that each time he appeals to the people he regards their vote as a real confirmation of his acts; and the fact that the government has a vast advantage over the opposition, in holding a virtual monopoly of the telecommunications media, does not diminish his conviction. Moreover, even if there were complete freedom of opinion, all demonstrations of popular sentiment hitherto would have supported him. The plausibility of plebiscites, therefore, depends upon the circumstances of the given case; under some circumstances the techniques of direct democracy are no more than lip service to democratic ideology. Despite all this, however, Max Weber was probably the first to clearly see the alternatives of plebiscitary or parliamentary methods of selecting political leadership.[40]

---

[40] See below, pp. 63 ff.

7. *Political Parties*

Max Weber defines political parties as "in their essence organizations voluntarily created and based on free recruiting which must be constantly renewed."[41] A further aspect of such parties is "a permanent cadre of party affiliates organized under a leader or group of notables" which is in charge of party finances, formulation of the program, presentation of candidates for electoral offices, and the strategy and tactics of party work. The modern party, therefore, is an apparatus which has created a fully trained bureaucracy of functionaries for its special purposes. Furthermore, it is organized on an oligarchic basis. The masses of the party voters have no share at all in framing its program or selecting candidates, and party members participate only marginally.

Edmund Burke as early as at the end of the eighteenth century had pointed out the fundamentally voluntaristic nature of the process by which parties are formed. Probably borrowing from M. Ostrogorski, Max Weber extended the definition to include a professionally operated organization, an apparatus of functionaries ranging from party headquarters to the ward clubs. He repeatedly made the point that contemporary national parties had their origin in the English caucus system.[42]

Nowadays it may seem platitudinous to assert that under conditions of mass democracy an apparatus of functionaries is indispensable for a political party. Then, however, it called for remarkable foresight to thus pass sentence on the parties directed by notables, which were still to be found everywhere in Europe, though no longer in England. Due to universal suffrage, all such parties have disappeared. "Bureaucratization of and financial planning by the parties are the concomitants of democratization."[43] The political requirements of mass democ-

---

[41] See *Staatssoziologie*, pp. 51 ff.; *Pol. Schr.*, p. 312.
[42] See, e.g., *Pol. Schr.*, pp. 523 ff.
[43] *Pol. Schr.*, p. 375.

racy, with its huge army of voters, can be met only by a rationally operated party apparatus, by the party "machine," whose functionaries have made politics their profession. In this connection,[44] Weber pointed out that legal procedures can determine the composition of the "party cadre." He may have been referring to the American technique of using primaries, as they were at that time, for selecting not only candidates for office but also party functionaries, for his knowledge of American political life was astounding.

Perhaps the lasting value of Max Weber's contributions to this subject was his prediction of the inexorable enlargement of the party apparatus and bureaucracy. To Weber this was only one more instance of the general tendency toward bureaucratization which he saw in all of society;[45] for in the mass state, electoral success depends on the rationalization of party recruiting. Effective party propaganda must be carried on by full-time functionaries, who are separate from the party leadership proper. Up to Weber's time the technical work of party organization was carried on by notables, more or less as a sideline. Weber foresaw that such methods would no longer be adequate. The establishment and direction of the party press and the handling of the party finances are part of the job of rationalizing the party machinery. And of particular importance is eliminating freedom of decision on the part of party deputies in the parliaments. In the liberal era such freedom, deriving from Burke's ideas, had become habitual. Its place has been taken by the submission to party goals in the form of strict party discipline. The process of running a party also involves the creation of youth organizations, setting up schools for party officials and speakers, and, most important, cementing ties with economic interests friendly to the party. Examples of the latter are the partnerships, common today, between parties and certain economic associations—the socialists

---

[44] *Staatssoziologie,* p. 52.
[45] See *Pol. Schr.,* pp. 372 ff.

with the trade unions, say, and the bourgeois parties with the employers' organizations.

Although the evolution toward bureaucratization was still in its initial stages in Weber's day, it has since continued and become fully consolidated, exactly as he foresaw. Under the impact of universal suffrage, all parties in present-day mass democracy have become gigantic party machines which function by their own momentum, independent of state regulation. The masses of voters swayed by the mass media are nothing but a herd, cannon fodder for the strictly oligarchic party directorates. It is true that recent constitutions—those of the German Federal Republic, Italy, and the USSR—have undertaken to recognize the parties as official institutions, necessary components of the machinery of state. But no country has achieved real legal regulation of the party dynamics.[46] Even American efforts to impose internal party democracy by law, as in the above-mentioned primaries, have come to naught. Only the socialist parties have a chance, as M. Duverger has recently shown, to exert some degree of control over the autonomous party oligarchy by strict observance of party statutes. The real dynamism of parties—the struggle for the spoils of power—cannot be contained in juridical formulas. It must remain anarchic, in a state of unregulated liberty. Here, too, Max Weber proved perfectly prescient.

Weber also maintained that the multiparty system of his time would necessarily and naturally continue in the European industrial countries of the future.[47] His prediction came true for all

---

[46] See Karl Loewenstein, "The Legal Institutionalization of Political Parties," in *Extrait des rapports généraux au Ve congrès international de droit comparé* (Brussels: Établissements Émile Bruylant, 1959), pp. 743 ff.

[47] *Pol. Schr.*, p. 372. Here Weber predicts four or five sizable political parties, with the concomitant need for coalition governments. His prediction proved valid for Weimar and, with certain reservations, for Bonn also.

European continental states until the eruption of totalitarianism. The two-party system in Great Britain and the old Dominions—which has recently begun to break down, as in Canada—is based on altogether different traditions and national psychologies. We may note in passing that Max Weber's prediction has not been invalidated by Bonn's apparent approach to the two-party system. The totally anti-democratic five per cent clause has helped to simplify the party structure by eliminating smaller parties in Germany; but four larger party combinations have nevertheless survived, just as Weber foresaw. A genuine party of the right has not yet arisen, and could only do so at the expense of the government party, the CDU, which has held power since 1949. Similarly, a split in the Socialist Party, the SPD, can be avoided only as long as the ban on the Communist Party is maintained.

All parties that have once been organized and integrated into political life display an amazing tenacity of life. Wherever freedom to form new parties is restored after a thoroughgoing change in regime—as in Germany in 1918 and 1945, France and Italy after 1945—the former parties reappear on the scene, often without even troubling to change their personnel or acquire new labels. So-called landslides, always a possibility in general elections, have been relatively rare—examples are those of the Nazis in 1930 and of the short-lived Poujadists in France in 1952. It remains to be seen whether these principles will prove true in France when the de Gaulle period has come to its end.

On the other hand, Max Weber's notions about patronage in the American parties have been largely outmoded by later developments. As we have shown,[48] the introduction of the Civil Service system for most official positions has strictly limited the opportunities for patronage available to the victorious party. In addition, the two parties have by now shed their ideological differences to such an extent that they appear basically to be the

---

[48] See above, p. 38.

two wings of a single middle-class party, engaged in the struggle for political power purely for its own sake.[49]

We may be inclined to question Max Weber's fundamental distinction between patronage parties and ideological parties.[50] All political parties practice patronage insofar as they aim at placing their leading politicians in key government posts. In coalition governments, instead of the victorious party's monopoly of offices, there is a distribution of ministerial posts, including those of the ministerial bureaucracy, among the partners forming the coalition. The Bonn government provides a clear, though by no means gratifying, example for this kind of horse-trading. All-party governments which divide up the spoils among themselves and thus run counter to the supreme aim of politics—the struggle for political power—are exceptional and scarcely ever of any degree of permanence. The most striking examples of such are Austria from 1945 to 1966 and Colombia since 1958.

Since the Second World War, and since all countries have begun to transform themselves as much as possible into welfare states, political parties have everywhere begun to shed the ideological differences that previously attracted voters to them. At the moment, party programs really differ only over the matter of what share of the economy is to be assigned to the public, what share to the private sector. Basically, the differences consist in how much leeway should be left to the latter. To be sure, the Catholic parties are still ideologically oriented. They have long been present in Germany, Switzerland, Holland, and Belgium; and since Weber's time they have also emerged in Italy (after the First World War), in France after the second war, and recently in Latin America—Argentina, Chile, and elsewhere. But

---

[49] Max Weber could not, of course, foresee that the Democrats would be split by the Negro question, nor that boss rule of the parties, a factor he often reverted to, has virtually vanished today.

[50] *Pol. Schr.*, pp. 312 f.

thanks to the social philosophy of the Vatican, these parties too have entered the Elysian fields of the welfare state. The socialist parties no longer make much of their class structure and the class struggle; the ideological disagreements with their bourgeois rivals have been largely abandoned, and they have made rapid progress in adopting middle-class ways of thinking.

In the place of contrasting party ideologies, a kind of uniform ideology has arisen which no nation and no party can escape— including, especially, communism. We have already alluded to this: its two cardinal goals are to raise the standard of living for the masses and to attain a greater degree of social justice for underprivileged strata of the population. Even the tensions between West and East ultimately come down to disagreement over the methods by which a higher standard of living for all may be achieved.[51]

Max Weber repeatedly insisted that politics amounts to conflict and that the political parties wage a struggle for political power. He has been proved perfectly right. Political parties today are merely bureaucratically administered and rationally conducted organizations fighting for political power. The ideological infrastructure that once differentiated them has shrunk to campaign promises: each pledges that it will do better than the others in improving the national standard of living.

In retrospect, Max Weber seems to have erred on two counts: his view of the necessarily voluntaristic nature of parties and his assumption that the existence of competing parties in a mass state is indispensable and inevitable. These were the ideas of a liberal still rooted in the nineteenth century. The revolutionary innovation in the political situation of our time is the totalitarian state, which has transformed the typically liberal party based on voluntary adherence into the totalitarian party with compulsory membership. Freedom of party choice has been replaced by an al-

---

[51] See above, pp. 9 f.

most military subordination to the commands issued by the party leadership, which is identical with the leadership of the state. Under pressure of the mass media, the supposedly free-willed individual must obey their orders. Max Weber found no historical precedents for the one-party totalitarian state of either the Communist or Fascist brand. For although despotisms have always existed, none has been launched and maintained by a party —except for that prototype of the totalitarian party, the Jacobins. Factions have always existed: the Optimates and Populares at the end of the Roman Republic, the "circus parties" in Byzantium, the Bianchi and Neri in Republican Florence. But genuine parties are an invention of the nineteenth century, and in particular a product of mass democracy as it then took form. One may go so far as to deny any "party" character to the one-party state, since the very concept of party government implies the existence of several competing political parties. Max Weber could not foresee this turn of affairs. He could not know, and could scarcely have imagined, the effect upon individual and collective decisions of propaganda techniques monopolistically applied through the mass media by a governmental coercive apparatus. This replacement of a constitutional state, based on the citizen's voluntary submission to legally constituted power holders by a despotic state, in which rulers impose their will on powerless subjects—however they may camouflage the situation by pseudo-legitimate techniques of popular support—was one phenomenon of the present day that could not but escape Max Weber's foresight—and therefore left a gap in his typology of the possible forms of governmental patterns.[52]

---

[52] See below, pp. 88 ff.

IV. Plebiscitary Mass Democracy and Caesarism

1. The Plebiscitary Leader

The picture of plebiscitary mass democracy as the pattern of political organization and the manner in which it gives rise to the "Caesaristic" leader are central features of the Max Weber's political sociology.[1] Plebiscitary installation of the political leader is the expected, though not inevitable, consequence of full democratization through universal suffrage—through which the people have risen to the position of the power-holder in their own right. In this sense mass democratization brings with it a method of selecting political leaders which is supplementary to and, in some cases, a substitute for the parliamentary designation. "The political leader . . . attains leadership . . . by winning the loyalty and confidence of the masses, in his person and his power, by demagogic means addressed to the masses. In the nature of things this means the resort to a Caesaristic method of selecting political leadership."[2] It is obvious that an established parliament will do its best to fight such dangerous competition—as, for example, the French Third Republic successfully did in the Boulanger crisis (1889). By contrast, the Fourth Republic was unable to check de Gaulle's "legal" coup d'état of 1958. But in the long run parliamentary government cannot hold

---

[1] *Pol. Schr.*, pp. 381 ff.
[2] *Pol. Schr.*, p. 382.

out against an irresistible tendency. The political parties especially must sail with the plebiscitary wind; because of the Caesaristic aspects of mass democracy, they have no choice but "to accept as leaders persons with real political temperaments and gifts as soon as such persons prove capable of winning the confidence of the masses."[3]

Such insight indicates Max Weber's truly uncanny sense for the shape of things to come. Everywhere in our age of mass democracy the political leader dominates the scene, chosen either by the legitimate plebiscitary method of the ballot or by "acclamation" as its pseudo-legitimate substitute. There is scarcely a political society—except, perhaps, for the marginal few in which remnants of traditional rule survive—that has been able to escape this universal tendency. That applies equally to old-established states which as yet have found no stable political form and to the new, unstable, developing states which have turned to neo-presidentialism in disguised or undisguised form.

England,[4] among the older constitutional democracies, has exemplified the plebiscitary trend for nearly a century. When the voter goes to the polls, he hopes to see a particular leading personality emerge as victor of the election. The voter is motivated primarily by the personal element, and his preference for a particular political party is expressed by his vote for its publicly acknowledged leader.[5] This plebiscitary component in the British general elections seems to have persisted even during the exist-

---

[3] *Pol. Schr.,* p. 391.

[4] *Pol. Schr.,* pp. 282 f. and 522 ff. Here, however, Weber judges Gladstone—who in the Midlothian, an electoral campaign of 1879, introduced plebiscitary elements into the English two-party system—more favorably than would present-day political scientists.

[5] The postponement of long overdue new elections in Great Britain until October, 1964 was dictated by the Conservatives' need to build up the "image" of the new and hitherto unknown Prime Minister, Sir Alec Douglas-Home, in order to make him attractive to the mass of the electorate.

ence of the three-party system, when there was no either-or choice between two party leaders.

Strict parliamentary selection of leaders, then, has been maintained only in those old-established parliamentary states in which the existing multiparty system has necessitated coalition governments (Belgium, Holland, the Scandinavian countries), and the electorate thus had no clear choice among leader-personalities. On the other hand, in the Federal Republic of Germany the personal-plebiscitary character of elections held up to the present (a character which the government party in particular has skillfully exploited in its propaganda) has been founded on the two-party alternative that has again and again been impressed upon the voters. In the United States, whose government is not parliamentary, because Congress is shorn of the power of designating the president, the plebiscitary nature of elections is built into the constitution. Motivations conditioned by the preference for a specific candidate are so much in the ascendancy that many of the voters abandon their party attachment for the politically more attractive presidential candidate. This tendency is reinforced by the fact that the party programs have become almost indistinguishable from one another. Thus the presidential election of 1960 shaped up as primarily a battle between Kennedy and Nixon and only secondarily between Democrats and Republicans. In the presidential campaign of 1964 between Johnson and Goldwater, the personal-plebiscitary factor shaped the outcome of the election even more than in the past, because the Republican Party did not stand united behind its official candidate.

In countries under authoritarian leadership, finally, a parliament may either be kept going for the sake of appearance or may have been completely abolished. Be this as it may, the plebiscitary choice of leaders has today become altogether indispensable and provides the sole "legitimation" of open or masked dictatorship. Plebiscites on dictatorial-authoritarian constitutions, or to "elect" a dictator already in power, or for similar purposes, have become the standard pseudo-democratic mummery of contemporary despotism. There can be no question of genuine "selection" of political leadership in such situations, for only a single candidate, supported by the tanks and machine guns of his prætorian guard, is "running" for office. The election has degenerated to the registering of acclamation. Thus the plebiscitary leader must always be a "tribune of the people."[6]

Nowadays we have more reason to be skeptical of plebiscitary selection of leaders than Max Weber could possibly be. As long as a constitution remains in force, absolute majorities, if they happen at all in honest elections, are exceedingly rare. Not even Hitler attained a majority in the elections of March 1933, which were formally still tolerably honest, although terrorism certainly affected the outcome. Nevertheless, he received only 43.9% of the vote. We need not speak of Mussolini's shameless manipulation of the electoral process. When the small fry among contemporary dictators boast of their famous 99%, we know that there has been outright falsification of the results of the elections. In the primitive milieu of most developing countries, where fraud is rampant, genuine plebiscites simply do not take place. The art of controlling political decisions at the polls also has to be learned, although this is a subject which attracts many apt pupils.

As Max Weber has shown, there is an inseparable link between the plebiscitary selection of leaders and the demagogism inherent in mass democracy.[7] "Since the establishment of the constitutional state, and even more so since the inauguration of democracy, the demagogue is the type of the leading politician in the Occident."[8] As a sociologist, Weber had no illusions: "Democracy and demagogy belong together. An idealization of the realities of life would be pointless self-deception." And again:

---

[6] Max Weber, however, nowhere employed this expression.

[7] *Pol. Schr.*, pp. 379 ff., 513 ff.

[8] *Pol. Schr.*, p. 513.

"The demagogue rises to the top, and the successful demagogue is the man who is the most unscrupulous in methods of propaganda."[9] Who, reading this sentence today, fails to think of the monster of the recent past who wielded the Big Lie with such daemonic virtuosity that he owed his seizure of power to it? To Max Weber, however, the concept of the demagogue was without moral connotation and was strictly utilitarian. He classified as demagogues both Pericles and the classical textbook example, the dyer Cleon.[10] It would follow that any plebiscitary leader of our time—a Macmillan, a Kennedy, an Adenauer, a de Gaulle—would have to conduct himself demagogically in order to come to or to stay in power in a full democracy. In the present-day democratic mass state, no leader can rise to the top unless he is a demagogue.[11]

But it is precisely the nature of constitutional democracy that it can set limits to and neutralize the effects of demagoguery. This is proved by the examples of England[12] and of other constitutional democracies such as the United States. The "established legal forms of political life" are able to minimize the impact of demagoguery, especially when the leader of the masses moves "within the fixed organization of the parties" and is forced to "school and prove himself by participating in the committee work of the parliament, regulated as that is by established conventions." Thus constitutional democracy is by no means, he holds, at the mercy of demagoguery. But Weber could not, of course, imagine that the master demagogues of our times—the

---

[9] The two quotations above are from *Pol. Schr.*, p. 379.

[10] *Pol. Schr.*, p. 513.

[11] Max Weber speaks (*Pol. Schr.*, p. 392) of the "present irrational rule of the streets typical of purely plebiscitary nations" and suggests that his Germans were immune to this sort of thing. Had he lived, he would have been bitterly disappointed; for both the seizure of power by the Nazis and their subsequent hold was founded upon "rule of the streets" manipulated from above.

[12] *Pol. Schr.*, p. 391.

Hitlers, Mussolinis and their ilk—as sworn enemies of parliamentarism would on principle abstain from parliamentary deliberations and would rise solely by demagogic appeals to the masses. De Gaulle, too, belongs to this category of anti-parliamentary demagogues.

2. The Caesaristic Leader

Max Weber outlined the logical stages by which the plebiscitary leader becomes transformed into the Caesaristic leader.[13] The technical term "Caesarism" is derived from Gaius Julius Caesar, who won absolute power in the period of the Roman Republic's fatal decline by assuming all the leading offices in the state, in defiance of the republican constitution. Caesar persuaded emotionalized and largely corrupted popular assemblies to grant him these offices beyond the restricted legal term and even for his lifetime. Thus he could aver the legitimacy of his absolute rule, the properly constituted organs of the Republic having voted him legal dictatorship. The fiction of the *lex regis de imperio* prevailed throughout the principate as the basis of the legitimate exercise of power by the *princeps*. The nineteenth century gave a good deal of attention to the phenomenon of Caesarism, though it went by the name of Bonapartism, after its most recent precedent (Roscher, Treitschke, Bagehot).

The identity between the plebiscitary and the Caesaristic leader lies, according to Max Weber, in the use of the plebiscite as the basis of power. A plebiscite "is no ordinary vote or election, but a declaration of 'faith' in the vocation for leadership of the person who claims this acclamation for himself."[14]

We must raise certain objections to Max Weber's use of the term "Caesarism." He applies it rightly to the two Napoleons. But he also applies it repeatedly[15] to Bismarck, a man rather of

---

[13] *Pol. Schr.*, pp. 381 ff.
[14] *Pol. Schr.*, p. 382.
[15] E.g., *Pol. Schr.*, pp. 335, 382.

his own stamp, for whom he felt an ambivalent love-hatred. To be sure, Bismarck's dominance may have been "Caesaristic" in its extent; but he certainly owed it to the confidence of his monarch rather than to popular vote. Thus he lacked entirely the typically Caesaristic legitimation; he was not the people's choice.

In addition, it is open to question whether the plebiscitary leader always and in all circumstances conducts himself Caesaristically, that is, that there are no limits upon the exercise of his power. Since Weber's day, to be sure, a number of political leaders who achieved power by plebiscitary methods have exercised it absolutely, without constitutional limitations—men such as Hitler, Mussolini, Nasser and, with some reservations, General de Gaulle. But the material for comparative studies has swelled greatly since Weber's day and makes it apparent that plebiscitary and Caesaristic leaders are not necessarily identical. We have also learned that a leader chosen by more or less plebiscitary techniques may nevertheless be integrated into the parliamentary system—as the example of England shows.

Whether a plebiscitary leader in office acts as a Caesar depends on the political milieu in which he came to power. Franklin D. Roosevelt certainly had a strong plebiscitary basis for his power. Yet neither he nor, say, Macmillan, felt or behaved like new Caesars. Erlander, the Social Democratic Prime Minister of Sweden, has enjoyed steady popular support since 1946; yet there is certainly nothing Caesaristic about his management of Swedish political life. In original Caesarism and in its subsequent forms the lack of constitutional counterbalancing factors permitted an unlimited exercise of power. There were no constitutional safeguards of the sort we find in the present-day governments of Great Britain and the United States, nor was there any regular procedure for curbing the Caesars without resorting to force. As long as constitutional democracy is really functioning, the constitution itself presents even the strongest executive with insurmountable obstacles and prevents it from slipping into

Caesaristic dictatorship. Of such nature are the conventions of the British Constitution, which are binding on every prime minister, no matter how large his electoral majority. Of such nature also are the checks and balances built into the separation of powers in the American Constitution. And in the political environments of both countries, the courts are the greatest shield against Caesarism. In the United States, moreover, the Twenty-second Amendment (1951) which restricts a president to two terms in office has barred any legal perpetuation of presidential power.[16]

Obviously, the core of the whole question is whether there is a legal way for removing a political leader who has come to power by plebiscitary means, once he has lost the confidence of the masses, and thus what Weber calls his "test" of legitimacy. For the essence of Caesarism consists in the impossibility of

---

[16] Wolfgang J. Mommsen in his otherwise excellent book, *Max Weber und die deutsche Politik 1890-1920* (Tübingen: Mohr, 1959), several times (e.g., pp. 140, 143, 200 f.) maintains that in advocating a popularly elected president under the Weimar Constitution, Max Weber was exchanging an outmoded form of democracy for the new, plebiscitary "leader democracy" and thus contributed toward "psychologically preparing the German people for acclamation of Adolf Hitler's leadership." This hypothesis completely misreads the position of the president of the Weimar Republic. In fact, the president was constitutionally so limited (he could even be recalled by the people in conjunction with the parliament) that a "plebiscitary leader-state" could not possibly have arisen through any action on his part. What is more, Mommsen's thesis completely misunderstands Max Weber's political ethics. Such a distortion could not go unchided (see Karl Loewenstein, "Max Weber als 'Ahnherr' des plebiszitären Führerstaats," in *Kölner Zeitschrift für Soziologie und Sozialpolitik*, vol. 13 [1961], pp. 275 ff.; see also Mommsen's feeble and unsubstantiated attempt at a justification, *ibid.*, vol. 15 [1963], pp. 295 ff.). This perversion of Weber's thought would not be worth mentioning if Mommsen and others had not repeated the denigration (if newspaper accounts are to be believed; see *Süddeutsche Zeitung*, No. 107 of May 7, and *Frankfurter Allgemeine Zeitung*, No. 195 of May 8, 1964) in addressing the Heidelberg congress of sociologists. As Goethe says, "Getretener Quark wird breit, nicht stark," which might be rendered into American: "No matter how you slice it, it's still baloney."

putting a legal end to absolute rule. Max Weber keenly perceived the crux of the problem and explained it in terms of the example of England: "Parliament is the constitutional limiting framework for the holder of constitutional power, guaranteeing the stability as well as setting the limits for the prime minister's exercise of power. He cannot infringe upon the guaranteed rights of the citizens. The internal machinery of Parliament provides an 'orderly form of political testing' and, above all, peaceful elimination of the Caesaristic dictator when he has lost the confidence of the masses."[17]

We cannot, therefore, completely accept Max Weber's opinion —provided he really held it—that the plebiscitary leader is always the Caesaristic leader. Nevertheless, the matter involves a problem of great importance which becomes apparent only in retrospect, from our present vantage point. How, we must ask, in a political environment in which the established techniques of constitutional democracy do not operate, can a leader who has come to power by plebiscitary means and exercises it Caesaristically be unseated? In constitutional democracy, where the political rules of the game are respected equally by the leaders and the led, periodic general elections solve the problem; the plebiscitary call can be rescinded by plebiscitary recall. But once the plebiscitary leader has entrenched himself by Caesaristic exercise of power, the normal constitutional methods of recall do not function—assuming that they really exist and are not just semantic frauds. The Caesar cannot be deposed by the constitution because he himself is the constitution. The masses of the people or of the voters do not cling to him because he consistently proves that he can satisfy their desires or needs. Rather, he and his henchmen so completely dominate the coercive apparatus of the state that the people no longer have the means of showing

---

[17] *Pol. Schr.*, p. 383. It is certainly an exaggeration to characterize the British Prime Minister as a Caesaristic dictator, except in wartime, which is what Max Weber may have been thinking of at that time.

their loss of faith in him. They cannot get rid of him without violence. As Machiavelli foresaw, the "armed prophet" who employs coercion to put across his innovations is wholly superior to the "unarmed" one. The crowd is fickle; the Caesaristic leader must therefore have the means to force it to fidelity when it no longer believes in him and his mission.[18] The new Machiavellians have faithfully followed this prescription. The coercive instruments of the state—either the armed forces of the generals or the leader's prætorians, together with the opinion-forming mass media—are exclusively at the Caesaristic dictator's disposal. As long as he controls them, he can compel the people to believe in him and his exercise of power remains unassailable. Hence the reign of a Caesaristic dictator can be brought to an end only by his death, by a revolution which is successful because the armed forces desert him, by outside intervention, or by defeat in war.

We need only consider the political situation in de Gaulle's France to see a textbook example of the symbiosis between a plebiscitary power-base and Caesaristic authority. The constitution provides for strong presidential powers. Traditional liberties have more or less survived; but the parliament and the political parties have been so weakened, and the government so completely controls the vital telecommunications, that an effective

---

[18] The stinging passage from Chapter VI of *Il Principe* (*Le Opere Maggiori di Niccolò Machiavelli*, Florence: Sansoni, 1934, pp. 27 f.) is pertinent here for its remarkable contemporaneity: "Di qui nacque che tutti profeti armati vinsono, e li disarmati ruinorono. Perchè, oltre alle cose dette, la natura dei populi è varia; ed è facile a persuadere loro una cosa, ma è difficile fermarli in quella persuasione; *e pero conviene essere ordinato in modo que quando non credono più si possa fare creder loro per forza.*" (Thus it comes about that all armed prophets have conquered and unarmed ones have failed; for besides what has been already said, the character of peoples varies, and it is easy to persuade them of a thing, but difficult to keep them in that persuasion. *And so it is necessary to order things so that when they no longer believe, they can be made to believe by force.*" (Italics mine.)

opposition has become virtually impossible—at least for the time being. Paradoxically, this has been proved, rather than disproved, by the presidential elections of late 1965: though President de Gaulle had been forced into a second ballot, the combined opposition was not strong enough to deny him the second term.

Historical studies had convinced Max Weber that Caesaristic authority needs more than a plebiscitary base; it must control the coercive apparatus of the state in order to nip all opposition in the bud, and it must monopolize the means of influencing public opinion. He could not, however, foresee the potential of the mass media for producing unresisting conformity. For Weber, the press and public meetings were still the principal means of shaping public opinion. Today, the electronic mass media, the most beneficent and most diabolical invention of the last half-century, hammer the image of the leader into the masses and overwhelm the appeal of all competing forces. If necessary, the apparatus of the government party, likewise dominated by the leader, can be pressed into service.

Under this same heading come all those only too well known coercive and terroristic techniques of dictatorial regimes such as the ban on free parties, compulsory membership in the single government party, repression of all activity regarded by the regime as subversive, penalties for listening to radio broadcasts hostile to the regime, and numerous others *ad nauseam*. Together with the skillful glorification of the leader and his achievements, these methods create a climate in which neither individual nor collective rebellion is possible as long as the military chiefs identify with the leader-dictator—whether for reasons of class egoism, class privilege, or patriotism.

This is the characteristic development of our time which only the old-established western democracies (France excepted) have been able to escape; it could not really be foreseen by Max Weber, scion of the reason-oriented nineteenth century that he was. Time has invalidated his optimistic view[19] that the traditional constitutional order and the "firmly organized" parties would serve to hold in check the plebiscitary leader's Caesaristic aspirations. Frequently the constitutional order has been either eliminated or given a dictatorial twist; and political parties have been undermined by newly formed "personalistic" revolutionary parties to such a degree that they have been emptied of all meaning. And everywhere the instrument to bring about these changes has been potential or actual terror. The nineteenth century with its "legitimate" investiture in power has been followed by the twentieth with its illegitimate usurpation.

3. The Charismatic Leader

In the whole of Max Weber's political sociology, the concepts that, to all intents and purposes, had the greatest impact on the thinking of our time are those of *charisma* and the *charismatic leader*.[20] The word and the idea have entered the everyday language of politics.

With Weber we now recognize three types of rule: legal rule based on established norms, traditional rule by custom, and charismatic rule based on devotion to a leader whose gifts are considered supernatural and exceptional. Max Weber drew upon his prodigious knowledge of history to work out these fundamental types, and this system of types is rightly considered his essential contribution to political sociology.

Great leaders do, of course, emerge among rulers by legal and by traditional authority, a fact which Max Weber was certainly mindful of. But he regards the charismatic type as embodying the leader truly destined to rule. Such leaders may appear as prophets, war heroes, demagogues in the Greek *ecclesia*,

---

[19] *Pol. Schr.*, p. 391.

[20] See "Die drei reinen Typen der legitimen Herrschaft," in *Staatssoziologie*, pp. 104 ff. and *Pol. Schr.*, pp. 495 ff.

or in parliaments. "The frame within which authority operates integrates the society and its members."[21] The followers obey the leader because of his extraordinary qualities. But the charismatic bond between leader and the led endures only as long as the leader's charisma is verified by miracles, successes, material benefit to his followers or subjects—in other words, only as long as he is the ruler "by the grace of God."[22] We cannot here delve into the further questions that Max Weber discusses in this context: succession in charismatic authority and the "routinization" of charisma.

In the light of our own, only too often painful experiences since Weber's day, we must consider how the concepts of plebiscitary, Caesaristic, and charismatic leaders are interrelated. Furthermore, we must ask whether the category of the charismatic actually is as fundamental as Max Weber assumed.

One may start out with the observation, contained within the concept, that a Caesaristic leader must always come to power by plebiscitary techniques, either by free election or by acclamation which in substance is tantamount to election. The consensus of the people is essential for the legitimation of his rule. True Caesarism, therefore, is conceivable only in that historically limited milieu in which the democratic ideology is accepted. The express or implied will of the people alone provide the legitimate base for a Caesar's rule. Historically, then, the plebiscitary ruler could come to power only in Greece and ancient Rome, in Byzantium (if we will accept the Byzantine custom of acclamation by the populace of the capital as manifestation of the popular will), and finally in the constitutional states of the West after the Puritan, American, and French revolutions. This localization, which of course confines the concept within narrow historical limits, is essential. Otherwise, "Caesarism" loses meaning and becomes the label for any kind of absolute rule.

---

[21] *Staatssoziologie,* p. 104.
[22] *Ibid.,* p. 106.

The charismatic leader, on the other hand, *may* have come to power by plebiscitary legitimation, but he does not *have* to have done so. Plebiscitary acquisition of power is, therefore, no absolute prerequisite to charismatic rule. Charismatic and plebiscitary elements may and often do cooperate, since the magic the leader radiates influences his selection and may be translated into votes. On the other hand, the plebiscitary leader need not possess charismatic qualities. Should he have them, so much the better for him; they strengthen his claim to popular legitimation.

Furthermore, absolute rule—"Caesaristic" only in the figurative sense, according to its effects, but not in the strict sense of Max Weber's concept—can be attained entirely without plebiscitary legitimation, and above all without charismatic motivation on the part of the ruled. Numerous examples of this can be cited from both past and present. Absolute rule may be won by infiltration and subversion of existing regimes, by coup d'état from above, by revolution directed from above or arising "spontaneously," and above all by the use of illegitimate violence. Under this last heading fall the military dictatorships so common nowadays. These may be naked military despotisms, or they may be disguised as civilian governments; they may resort, after they have been installed by force, to the formal legitimation of a manipulated plebiscite. But it would be exceedingly difficult to discover in most of the more recent dictatorial regimes any genuine plebiscitary legitimation, let alone the least trace of charismatic motivation. Almost without exception, these regimes began as movements by a minority.

All this comes down to the fact that neither genuine plebiscitary rule nor a "Caesaristic" regime of absolute force requires a charismatic infrastructure. We may even say that the attainment of rule by virtue of the charisma of a particular aspirant to power represents the exception and, to boot, a rare exception. Hence follows the necessity to re-examine what Max Weber meant by charismatic rule. Undoubtedly, the concept was a great stroke of genius, an event rare indeed in the social sciences. But will the category withstand strict scientific analysis?

It seems to us that the terms of plebiscitary, Caesaristic, and charismatic belong to different conceptual categories. The first two denote processes of *statecraft;* plebiscitary refers to the attainment of political power, Caesaristic to the exercise of the power attained by plebiscitary means. Charisma, on the other hand, belongs to the realm of what is nowadays called the *theory of influence;* it concerns the modes of behavior governing the mutual relationship of leader and following. Undeniably, charisma has its source in the person of the charismatic leader. But it can be effective only if it evokes a response from those to whom it is directed, that is, arouses belief in the leader's exceptional and supernatural mission. Charisma, then, is a category belonging to the disciplines of mass and social psychology. What motivations prompt the masses of the voters to give their allegiance to one leader rather than another? To answer questions such as these involves distinguishing the specific mysterious influence of charisma from other types of socio-psychological behavior in the struggle for political power.

What, then, constitutes the political leader's attractiveness for his voters or for "the people" in general? Is it inherent in his political opinions and intentions—in other words, in his "program"? Is it the "magical flow" of his eloquence? His mind, his knowledge, his experience? His demagogic talents? His identification with the *communis opinio,* of which he becomes the spokesman, or his opposition to it, in that he directs it along new paths? Whichever of these factors is present in a given case, we can say this: the political leader chosen by plebiscitary means must have qualities of popularity, or what we may more bluntly call political sex appeal. But popularity in itself does not yet constitute charisma. On the contrary, because it is so widely distributed it may interfere with charisma, which is—at least at first—an extremely personal interrelationship between the leader and the "initiates." We have enough empirical evidence by now to assume that very few of the plebiscitary leaders, in addition to their popular attractiveness, possess charisma. No one would claim that a British prime minister of modern times—not even Churchill, with his enormous popularity—has been graced with genuine charisma. The same can be said of American presidents, who undeniably possess plebiscitary legitimation. Certainly a political leader like Konrad Adenauer held a plebiscitary mandate. But to ascribe the mysterious quality of charisma to him would be perverting the very meaning of the word.

Naturally, it quite often happens that a mediocrity takes first rank in the political life of a nation.[23] Political mediocrities are sometimes useful and, on occasion, may be desirable, even necessary. In some countries, such as England or America, the masses actually fear brilliance, which contrasts too sharply with their image of themselves. We need only run down the list of British prime ministers or American presidents to confirm this observation. But there is one quality which must be possessed by the political leader in mass democracy, even if he is intellectually mediocre. That is personality, the one great basis for popularity. But once again, personality is by no means equivalent to charisma. Without positive qualities of personality no one can rise in politics these days. Formerly, in traditional forms of government where the sovereign's favor decided who would reach the top, neither personality nor popularity was essential. But in stating that popularity and personality are now prerequisites for political success, we have come no closer to the essence of charisma.

The verbal formulae of "charisma" and "charismatic authority" are so alluring, represent so original an "inspiration," that it is easy to neglect scientific analysis and use them where they do

---

[23] See *Pol. Schr.*, p. 380: "It sometimes happens that a mere rhetorician, without intellect and political character, acquires strong political power."

not apply. A felicitous coinage, in this case, may well become the *vertu des vices*.

First of all, we must keep in mind that the concept of charisma springs originally from the religious realm. As Max Weber freely admits,[24] Rudolf Sohm applied it to early Christianity; Weber borrowed the concept to transfer it to politics. Fundamentally, then, the locus of charisma is the world of religion. Probably all creators and shapers of religions had true charisma in some degree: Moses, Jesus, Mohammed, even Calvin and such founders of sects as Brigham Young. But in religion, charisma, as a gift of grace, flows from other sources than in politics; in religion its mainspring is faith, the conviction of the world beyond and the certainty of salvation.

We need not insist here on the distinctions that should be drawn between the phenomenon of religious charisma and political charisma. The dichotomy may be useful, however, because it raises the question of whether the quality of charismatic leadership is not peculiar, and always has been, to political milieus conditioned exclusively, or at least to a large extent, by magical, ritualistic, or mystically religious elements. If that were the case, charisma would apply chiefly to the pre-Cartesian West and, nowadays, to many parts of Asia and Africa which in spite of advancing rationalization only slowly are beginning to break away from the magico-religious ambiance. This may explain why reliable western observers attribute genuine charisma to certain African tribal chieftains who have risen, as the former colonies have achieved nationhood, to political leadership among their peoples: men like Nkrumah, Kenyatta, Nyerere, Kaunda, Mboya, and Dr. Banda. Their tribal followers regard these men as exceptionally and supernaturally gifted. This charisma is sustained essentially by the mystical and magical climate of the nonwestern environment. We may recall the position of the Japanese

---

[24] *Staatssoziologie,* p. 104.

Tenno before 1945; his prestige, stemming from a magical, ritualistic, religious tradition, simulated that of a charismatic leader. Western countries, however, have been subjected to the process of rationalization on which Max Weber laid so much stress. It may, therefore, be that in them the transference of the originally religious category of charisma to the political plane encountered far greater difficulties than in regions which, to use Kant's term, have not yet awakened from the "slumber of dogma." All these matters call for a careful investigation.

In addition, an important methodological problem arises. When we ascribe charisma to a political figure, we must distinguish between historical and contemporary examples. In regard to the great political leaders of the past who supposedly were gifted with charisma—Caesar, Augustus, Charlemagne, Cromwell, Gustavus Adolphus, Napoleon I, to name only a few —we of the present generation are dependent for our knowledge of their charismatic qualities upon the accounts of their contemporaries. But what do we know actually about Caesar? Did he really exude that supernatural magic, that gift of grace, which in Max Weber's terms constitutes the essence of charismatic authority? Perhaps—but the matter cannot be proved scientifically; certainly Shakespeare is no unimpeachable witness. We lack all standards and criteria for an objective judgment. We must not confound Caesar's timeless glory as one of the great political leaders with his immediate effect upon his contemporaries. And let us not forget that he was assassinated. Or, to mention Napoleon I (the third Napoleon, though far from commonplace, certainly had no charisma): we know infinitely more about Napoleon than we do about Caesar. In the years of his rise to power he surely seems to have had all the ingredients of charisma: the magic that emanated from him, the exceptional qualities that commanded utter devotion, his talent for projecting himself as an embodiment of idea and will. But after he became Emperor of the French, the office he held also exerted its influence upon people—Goethe not excluded—and the power connected with that office may have diluted the purity of the charismatic effect. Yet we must grant that even when aging and defeated he seems to have had command of some of the old magic; how else explain the memorable scene after Elba, when he confronted and won over the troops that had been sent out to arrest him?

Such examples might be multiplied at will, without securing a better insight into the essence of charisma. There is also a need for distinguishing between the dæmonic and the charismatic. Max Weber does not set up any category *sui generis* for the dæmonic; he apparently includes it within charisma. Yet the two need not be identical; we can well conceive of effective charisma devoid of any dose of the dæmonic element.

It is evident, then, that we can best detect and analyze the elements of true charisma in political leaders who are closer to our own time. But if we survey modern and recent history from this angle, we will discover scarcely any *political* figure to whom the concept of charisma can be fully or even partially applied. That may come as a great surprise if one happens to be under the persuasive influence of Max Weber's terminology. In the non-political realm, be it noted, the tensions and crosscurrents that make for charisma are by no means impossible. Stefan George, for example, may well have possessed charismatic authority; but in keeping with Max Weber's definition it was confined to the narrow circle of his "disciples," and outside that circle it faded away without leaving any traces. His charisma was altogether non-political and strictly personalized.

Among our contemporaries, charismatic magic appears to have existed in its strongest and purest form in Mahatma Gandhi. According to reliable accounts, no one who came near him could resist his spell. But in the first place, his charisma operated in a non-western milieu, and in the second place it was primarily religious in nature; the political influence associated with it was a side effect of the religious element. And Gandhi was assassinated.

Perhaps we ought also to consider his secular successor, Jawaharlal Nehru. In his best years Nehru may have had that incomprehensible quality that is called charisma. It was attested to not only by his fellow countrymen but also by all westerners who met him. But in Nehru, as well as Gandhi, the traditional religious and mystical elements were powerful allies in creating charismatic authority.

To pursue this matter further: Bismarck had the tremendous personality of the political leader, but certainly no charisma. Abraham Lincoln is so surrounded by legends that today it is scarcely possible to restore his original image. But there is much to suggest that he possessed charisma, and he, too, fell under the hand of an assassin. Franklin D. Roosevelt may have come closer to Weber's concept, but he still did not really fulfill it. Moreover, he had masses of enemies who were altogether immune to his spell. John F. Kennedy, removed prematurely from the political stage, undoubtedly had great personal charm and knew how to kindle a high degree of personal devotion among his young followers. But the majority of the Americans who voted for him would be amazed to be told that he had charisma. Personality and charm no more constitute charisma than does popularity.

To round off this discussion with two final examples concerning which everyone can form his own opinion. Hitler may certainly be regarded as a textbook example of a Caesaristic leader, who had come to power by plebiscitary means. Only pedants will raise the objection that he could not achieve a majority in the elections of March 1933—which, as we have already mentioned, were tolerably honest although held under conditions of mass terrorism. But did he also have what Max Weber would call charisma? Many of Weber's tests[25] of the charismatic ruler were present in the case of Hitler: the fanaticism he aroused in his adherents throughout his political career; the leader-follower relationship; authentication by "proofs"; selection of administrative staff on the basis of personal devotion, irrespective of technical qualifications or objective standards; and last but not least the demagogic mastery with which he proclaimed a nationalistic and racist ideology as a "revolutionary natural law." But did the man who embodied the "dictatorship of the corporals" that Max Weber predicted[26] also have the exceptional qualification of genuine charisma? After it was all over, a good many persons spoke of the magnetism of his deep blue eyes. But quite a few of those who knew him personally maintain that they noticed nothing of the kind. Whether or not Hitler represented an authentic example of charisma must, therefore, remain an open question until we have some scientifically verifiable standards for that quality.

To conclude this discussion with the contemporary, General de Gaulle. As far as can be surmised *ex post facto,* Max Weber would have respected de Gaulle as a patriot and courageous soldier but would have been repelled by his anachronistic pose of republican monarch and would have objected to his rank violations of the French constitution. Undoubtedly de Gaulle embodies the type of genuine plebiscitary leader, who, like a new Antaeus, has his legitimation confirmed by reiterated plebiscites and acclamations. Undoubtedly his hold on power and his conduct of government are genuinely Caesaristic. The lordliness with which he treats his own constitution is one prime demonstration of that. He towers above everyone around him, and no one would deny him the gift of political leadership. But can we attribute the quality of charisma to him? Does his magic extend beyond his subservient subordinates and aides and cast its spell upon the notoriously cynical French people? Far from it. The

---

25 *Ibid.,* p. 105.
26 *Pol. Schr.,* p. 280.

most malicious and biting jokes about him circulate. Could Gandhi have become the butt of popular derision? De Gaulle is useful to the French in these times, perhaps even indispensable. But their national pride, with its coloration of Cartesian rationality, would probably keep them from ever equating his prestige with charisma in Max Weber's sense. No one familiar with the mechanism of his plebiscites will have much doubt that what zealous legend-builders may represent as charisma is actually the result of extremely skillful manipulation of propaganda techniques. Not charisma, but a profound understanding of mass psychology and of all the tricks of demagoguery, is the basis of de Gaulle's popularity.

We must therefore ask whether Max Weber's category of the charismatic leader is perhaps not at all a universal and permanently valid type. Is it possibly confined to certain periods and milieus? Or to put this another way: in present-day technological mass society, in which the rules of democracy are consciously followed or at least acknowledged, is a charismatic basis of political rule at all possible and effective? To be sure, democratization has strengthened beyond all expectation the plebiscitary components in the power process; but at the same time it has decidedly diminished the chances for the development and operation of true charisma.

In earlier times, particularly before the invention of the printing press and before newspapers had become general instruments of opinion building, the personal magnetism of a political leader could be communicated only to the relatively limited number of persons with whom he came in direct contact. A Frederick II of Hohenstaufen (whom contemporaries significantly called *stupor mundi*), a Cromwell, or a Louis XIV were really known only to the relatively restricted group of their advisers, courtiers, officials, and soldiery. In their effect upon the masses of the people, the communication of the magical force of their personalities—charisma in the broader sense—was dependent upon transmission from mouth to mouth, which more often than not amounted to deliberate propagandizing from above. Very few subjects had ever seen their ruler face to face. They knew the leader's charisma only by repute and not by experience.

In the age of mass propaganda, in which the many media operate with the entire arsenal of subliminal psychology, the situation has changed fundamentally. Undoubtedly radio can reinforce the personal magnetism of the political leader and thus make an enormous contribution to his popularity, since only his eloquence, the quality of his voice—Roosevelt's secret weapon—is presented to the public. In television, on the other hand, his image is projected on the screen in every living room. Telecommunications, therefore, can give the personality of a leader an unprecedented mass effectiveness. Where the influence upon the masses depends on genuine charisma, radio and television can convey and solidify it to an extent unknown in all previous history. Paradoxically, however, modern mass technology diminishes rather than increases the spell of charisma. In technological mass society, with its visual and auditory propaganda techniques, political power is subjected to an irresistible process of personalization that brings rulers and ruled closer together than ever before. But the leader who shows himself daily—like Big Brother in Orwell's *1984*—is less magical and magnetic than the leader who is not seen at all, or only rarely on occasions especially favorable to him. Far from reinforcing charisma and spreading its magic in a wider context, the mass media in an open society act as disenchantments; this holds true not only for the skeptical intellectuals but for the masses as well. No one who lived in the United States during the so-called McCarthy era[27] will ever forget how rapidly the all-powerful Senator who dressed down generals like schoolboys, who had his fifth column in all the offices of the government, whose demagoguery reduced the administra-

---

[27] See Karl Loewenstein, *Verfassungsrecht und Verfassungspraxis der Vereinigten Staaten*, pp. 532 ff.

tion to helplessness, was toppled overnight. When the courageous director of a television network brought his behavior as
chairman of a Senatorial investigating committee before the eyes
of millions of viewers, the nightmare collapsed overnight. The
intimidated Senate was finally emboldened to censure McCarthy
severely, and thus put an end to his political career.

Such an effect applies, it is true, only to an open society in
which skepticism, criticism, and opposition function normally.
In a closed and authority-directed society, in which the organs of
propaganda are controlled by the supposed holder of charisma
and his subservient following, the mass media can produce a re-
enforcement and deepening of an originally spurious but arti-
ficially promoted charisma attributed to the ruler. In earlier
times, when communications were less advanced, charisma had
to be genuine to have lasting effects. But those effects can now
be conjured up by technological, rational methods, if the state
apparatus of coercion and propaganda is deliberately applied to
that end. It would appear that charisma, visualized in Max
Weber's system of categories as an independent substratum of
rulership, has become a victim of modern technology. In the
last analysis, as a basis of rule, it possesses a historical reality. Or,
to put it differently: charismatic authority in politics is a phenomenon of the pre-Cartesian world.

These observations, then, make it doubtful that the mysterious
vital fluid which unites the true charismatic leader with the
group devoted to him can develop at all in the present-day *political* environment. By no means, however, is this to imply that
charisma as a socio-psychological category of behavior and in-
teraction does not exist. The force of political charisma may have
been weakened in present-day mass society, for the reasons in-
dicated; but the reality of charisma as a human and social
phenomenon cannot be denied. Here, once again, experience
outweighs scientific skepticism. Limits have been set to their
political effectiveness; but charismatic personalities have always

existed and will always exist. Indeed, if the category is not restricted to political figures, they may occur more frequently than is generally assumed. To have met such personalities is a rare fortune to everyone who has the experience. Max Weber himself possessed to a high degree that exceptional gift of grace in which mind, knowledge, and character are united. Those of us whose path he crossed all became his "disciples" and succumbed to his "magic." He himself was the charismatic man he described.

To adduce another and more familiar example from our own times, of a person whose effectiveness in breadth and depth every professional politician would envy: Arturo Toscanini, as a conductor perhaps the greatest musical artist of this century, embodied charisma to a perfection attained by no other contemporary personality. In the language of the *Ode to Joy* that he performed so often and so magnificently, his magic united what stern fashion parted; under his baton all men became brothers: the musicians of the orchestra he conducted, the soloists who shared the platform with him, and the countless millions of the public who saw him face to face or partook of his perfect art on the radio or on records. No one could escape the magic of his musical and human personality. He was the charismatic person par excellence. But then, he was not a politician.

Yet another unique case comes to mind by which we are able to evaluate the genuineness of the charismatic phenomenon in the light of our living experience without having to rely on historical reports of its efficacy. Our generation was blessed by the presence in our midst—lamentably short as it turned out—of the saintly figure of Pope John XXIII. From his person a spell radiated of a purity of goodwill to all men and of humaneness that was felt spontaneously and deeply by the world far beyond the ecclesiastic oekumene. The impact was all the more universal since, stripped of all theological doctrine, it was articulated in the language of the common man. But perhaps it is just this last example that could induce us to do some rethinking on the entire complex of the charismatic. What the Holy Father incarnated in word and deed was simply human kindness in its ultimate perfection, devoid of any daemonic ingredients or even overtones that are commonly ascribed to the charismatic. Could it be that the charismatic, rather than being a category *sui generis,* is essentially identical with, or emanating from, those mysterious qualities that denote the great human personality?

4. The Typology of Legitimate Authority

Max Weber's elaboration of the three pure types of legitimate authority[28] is held to be his greatest achievement in political sociology. As historical categorization it has not lost its validity. If measured, however, both in terms of things to come and things that have come to pass, it seems to be the least satisfactory formulation of his socio-political frames, and the one that stands most in need of rethinking. Corresponding as it does to the state of knowledge in the nineteenth century, it is challenged by the facts of the twentieth century as we have experienced them.

Traditional rule, the first in Weber's classical trinity, "resting on the belief in the sanctity of immemorial arrangements and the submission to existing rule," has today, in this era of continuous world revolution, with its revaluation of all social and political values, survived in only a few regions of our shrunken globe. From the point of view of constitutionalism, these regions must be regarded as marginal. And even there, traditional authority is on the wane. The last bulwark fell with the collapse of Imperial Japan. This holds for both purely patriarchal rule—we need only consider the breakdown of tribal organizations among primitive peoples—and for the feudal structure of separate orders of society. Scarcely any traces of genuine political feudalism remain. The year 1789 was the watershed. The fading of politi-

---

[28] *Staatssoziologie,* pp. 99 ff.

cal authority, incidentally, as Weber clearly perceived,[29] is linked with the disappearance of the aristocracy as a ruling class.

Authority by established norms—what we would call today the constitutional state—was in the nineteenth century mankind's best hope for freedom and free fulfillment of the individual in a moral world-order. But in this twentieth century of illegal violence, the constitutional state has been forced on the defensive. After the First World War a sweeping wave of constitutional democracy overcame and replaced traditional authoritarianism in many countries. But now it has again lost much ground before the tide of social revolution and counterrevolution. This is evidenced by the upsurge of those new states within the Communist sphere that conform to the pattern which Georges Burdeau calls *démocratie gouvernée*. It is likewise proved by the military dictatorships, whether those that present a makeshift framework of social progressiveness, or those that are entirely without ideology, or those that are civilian despotisms based on support of the military. Only in the traditionally libertarian constitutional democracies of the European West, in North America, and in the sphere of influence of British political ideas, has the constitutional state been able to maintain itself and become more strongly integrated. The Federal Republic of Germany and Japan may be included in this group. Most of the states created since the Second World War accept only the shadow of constitutional democracy; very few of them practice its substance. This is not to say, of course, that the present state of affairs need be a permanent condition of mankind. On the contrary, one may have reason to hope that the frontiers of the democratic constitutional state will advance further into the political no-man's-land of dictatorship, once the latest wave of nationalism has ebbed and an encompassing organization of the world will permit a more just distribution of economic resources among the needy devel-

---

[29] *Pol. Schr.,* pp. 258 ff.

oping nations. Moreover, the signs that the Communist nations are moving toward constitutionality are too plain to be over-looked. But it is impossible to predict how long such an evolution may take; for despotism, no matter what its guise, has remarkable tenacity once it is established in power.

As for charismatic authority, we have already expressed our doubts about the continuing validity of the category in the age of technological mass democracy.

It seems, therefore, that Max Weber's typology of the patterns of rule needs to be expanded and complemented if it is to fit the contemporary experience. However, since Weber dealt only with *legitimate* authority, his framework must be extended to include a new category of illegitimate violence, since this is no less a type of *rule* than the legitimate patterns. A keen historian like Max Weber might have been able to trace the lineage of this new type of organization.[30] Or one might gain insight into the new category of illegitimate violence by using Guglielmo Ferrero's distinction between "legitimate" (monarchic or democratic) and "revolutionary" rule.[31] The salient characteristic of present-day tyranny or revolutionary authority is not so much that the rulers have seized power by force as that they sustain their position by monopolizing the state apparatus of coercion and total propaganda. Such an extension of Max Weber's typology would, however, have to be undertaken by a scholar who equalled Max Weber in historical knowledge and original creativeness. Given the uniqueness of Max Weber's genius, we shall probably have to wait a long time, if not in vain, for the appearance of such a successor.

[30] In connection with tyranny in the Hellenic world and the medieval Italian city-states, Max Weber stresses the illegitimacy of tyrannical rule, see *W.u.G.*, vol. II, pp. 787 ff. and 792 ff.

[31] See Guglielmo Ferrero, *The Principles of Power* (New York: G. P. Putnam's Sons, 1942), pp. 187 ff.

Epilogue

Personal Recollections of

Max Weber*

Your Magnificence! My colleague, the Honorable Minister Dr. Maunz! Fellow students! Ladies and Gentlemen!

I stand here as the representative of others who should rather have been called upon to deliver a memorial address on Max Weber. First among these I should mention your never-to-be-forgotten former President, Theodor Heuss; or the famous German philosopher who now lives in Basel, Karl Jaspers; or Georg Lukács, the important Marxist philosopher, who lives in Hungary. But since both the latter, because of age and other reasons, could not be asked here, the task of speaking to you today has fallen upon my frail shoulders.

I should begin by making certain reservations. Personally, I have tried to lead the life of a scholar, and a scholar does not talk about himself. He disappears behind his work. But it is in the nature of personal recollections that they must be presented in the first person singular.

My second reservation concerns the length of time that has elapsed since I first met Max Weber. On June 14 of this year, forty-four years will have passed since his death. Forty-four years is a long time in the life of a man, mine not excluded. It is also a long period in history. Those among you who are prepared to measure the passage of time in terms of historical eras may wish

---

* An address delivered at the University of Munich on June 3, 1964, on the occasion of the one hundredth anniversary of Max Weber's birth.

to reflect that forty-four years is longer than the period between the storming of the Bastille in July 1789 and the July Revolution of 1830; or, to choose an example closer to your own experience the period from the founding of the German Reich in 1871 to the outbreak of the First World War. These are long spans of time, and you must bear with the inevitable fallibility of my memory. You must also consider that I saw Max Weber when I was twenty, with the eyes and the idealism of youth. My image of Weber is a young man's image.

How did I come to meet him? The year was 1912. I had just passed the Bavarian intermediate state examination in law and had come to Heidelberg with the pride of that achievement and armed with a recommendation from the distinguished philologist Crusius, who was later to become president of the Bavarian Academy of Sciences and in whose home I had been a frequent visitor. Before I left for Heidelberg, he asked me whether I should like to meet Marianne Weber. She was, I knew, one of the leading proponents of women's rights in Germany and, moreover, something of a beauty. That was sufficient temptation for me to take up the offer gladly. The stupid young student that I was knew nothing of the existence of a husband named Max Weber.

My first weeks in Heidelberg were taken up with adjustment and with availing myself of the incredible opportunities for attending the lectures by the great scholars of those days. I may mention only Fritz Fleiner in constitutional law; Gustav Radbruch in criminal law; Ernst Tröltsch in the philosophy of religion; Hermann Oncken, the historian; Windelband, the great philosopher; and last but not least, Alfred Weber, brother of Max and then at the height of his fame. Several weeks passed, and it was about the beginning of June, the afternoon of a beautiful day, when I presented myself, introductory note in hand, at the house on the Ziegelhäuser Landstrasse to pay my respects to Marianne Weber.

Kea—she was the Webers' maid and ministering spirit, who spent her whole life with them and remained with Marianne after Max Weber's death—informed me that the Frau Professor was not in. Then, seeing my disappointment, she offered the consolation: "But if you like, you can see the Herr Professor."

Since I had come so far anyway, I thought I might just as well take a look at Herr Professor Weber. Kea led me into the garden. There, under the rose arbor, at a table heaped with books, sat Max Weber. He rose, greeted me, graciously invited me to sit down, and asked me a few of the usual questions. During our chat he must have noticed that I was interested in music, and what followed in the course of this first encounter with him was a wonderful and, for me, decisive revelation. For he began to block out a sociology of music for my benefit—this being a theme he was currently concerned with. I had thought that music flows from emotional and esthetic sources; and I now drank in his words as he explained that music, too, has rational and sociological foundations. He pointed out that the competition of the private capellas of princes and prelates in Italy, France, and Germany in the fourteenth and fifteenth centuries had had a distinct influence upon tonality; that hollow fifths, which were just then being heard again in Puccini's early operas, had been banished from music by the deliberate edict of a college of musicians in Florence; that the construction of musical instruments had influenced sonority and tonality; and, finally, that the tempering of the scale that was undertaken in the sixteenth and seventeenth centuries—for example by Johann Sebastian Bach in his *Well-tempered Clavichord*—had had rational and sociological motivations, and was not just the consequence of esthetic principles. I still recall his explaining to me the influence of the Greek modes, the Lydian, Phrygian, and Aeolian. Afterwards, whenever I heard the Lydian mode in one of the last Beethoven quartets, I thought of that first revelation I had received from Max Weber.

I must have sat with him for more than two hours. He was in the midst of work on the subject and obviously felt the need to articulate some of his thoughts. When at last I took my leave and went out on the road into one of those glorious Heidelberg June evenings, I was literally drunk. I was at a turning point in my life. From that moment on, I had taken the oath of fealty to him; I had become his vassal.

Perhaps I should say something about his appearance. He was tall, a head taller than I am, with heavy hair. His beard, already graying, covered two great dueling scars. His forehead was spiritualized—I can think of no other expression for it. His voice was a beautifully modulated baritone. He had a pair of eyes that could be kindly and critical almost simultaneously. To complete the picture I must add that his nose was of the variety rudely known as a pug nose. His speech was the most exquisite German I had ever heard up to that time, clear and measured, and entirely different from his writing style. For in writing the prodigality of his ideas repeatedly shattered the framework; he had more to say than he could really put into words.

Before I left, he invited me to come to the at-homes that were held every Sunday at his house from four o'clock on. I made use of that permission, both during that semester at Heidelberg and afterwards, for the at-homes drew me like a magnet back to Heidelberg. The *jours*, as the Webers called them, took place in the stately room on the second floor of the old house which had a ramp lined with vases of flowers leading up to it. Through the windows you looked across over the river at the Schloss with its red sandstone buildings. In the big room stood a life-size replica of the Charioteer from Delphi, and on the rear wall hung a magnificent painting by Karl Morgenstern, the father of the poet Christian Morgenstern. Its subject was the Gulf of Naples, and it lent a touch of southern brightness to the rather somber room.

At my first of these *jours*, I met Marianne Weber. She was

he soul of the circle, imperceptibly guiding, directing, balancing.
A lifelong friendship was to link me with her. After Max
Weber's death I visited her frequently in Heidelberg, and I
also had the honor to be her legal adviser in a number of matters. After the last world war, when I served in the American
military government, I saw her repeatedly again. She was a wonderful person, and the very partner that a great, volcanic, pas-
sionate man like Weber needed in daily life.

Among the regular visitors to those Sunday at-homes were
some of the foremost men in German intellectual life. But there
were three who were Max Weber's real interlocutors, to whom
he listened and with whom he had a genuine exchange of ideas.
These were Karl Jaspers, Georg von Lukács, and Friedrich Gun-
dolf. In the ritual that gradually developed on these Sunday
afternoons, these three in particular played the part of Weber's
friendly antagonists. When, after a while, the individual con-
versations had died down and we all gathered around Max
Weber, we would hear from his lips penetrating analyses of all
the subjects that concerned him and us—current events, questions of history and economics, philosophy, methodology, and a
great deal more. I do not think I am mistaken in saying that the
intellectual level of this select circle would have matched that of
the great salons toward the end of the Ancien Régime, or the
famous Berlin salons at the beginning of the nineteenth century.

Among those Sunday gatherings, one has remained in my
memory with peculiar force, that of July 26, 1914. It was a
gloriously lovely summer day. Austria had just declared war on
Serbia. It had not yet been decided whether Germany would enter
the war. But all of us knew that nemesis was moving irresistibly
down upon us. Our whole circle was there. Even those who attended infrequently had gathered to hear what Max Weber had to
say about the possibility of war and the prospects for the future. I
remember the whole scene as if it were yesterday. Weber was
profoundly pessimistic. He did not believe that the war would

be won "by the time the leaves fall," as the Kaiser shortly after
wards proclaimed rashly. He told us, and I remember his exac
words: "The war will last a long time; Prussian militarism i:
exceedingly tough." In this prediction he was of the same min
as three professionals; these were Chief of the German Genera
Staff von Moltke, a born pessimist; Joffre, the French Suprem
Commander, a born optimist; and British Field Marshal Lor
Kitchener, who knew war better than anyone else and foresav
that the Germans would fight to the last breath. Kitchener at th
time was counting on a war of some three years. Listening to th
conversation that Sunday, I had the feeling that I was where th
heart of Germany was beating.

I shall not say much more about subsequent meetings I ha
with Max Weber. In 1912 he came to Munich, the city he par
ticularly loved. Together we heard one of those enchantin
Mozart performances in the Residenztheater, *Così fan tutte* witl
Ivogün and Erb, conducted by Bruno Walter. Weber loved th
cityscape of Munich, the atmosphere of easygoing comfort an
intellectual sprightliness; and he had a humorous and smilin
understanding of the district called Schwabing, the Greenwicl
Village of Munich, which at that time was no geographical con
cept, but a spiritual no-man's-land where minds could meet an
whet each other.

I also want to say a few words about Max Weber's return tc
the lecture platform as a university professor and *praecepto*
Germaniae. When I met him in 1912 he was recovering from a
severe illness. In those days, no one was allowed to visit him in
the evenings, and he imposed the strictest regimen upon himself.
But he visibly improved, so much so that at the outbreak of the
war in 1914 he was able to do garrison duty as a reserve captain.
He was also appointed disciplinary officer of the Heidelberg
garrison, and afterwards he would often speak of how painful it
had been to have to send poor devils into the military stockade.

In the long run, such duties were not for him, and ultimately he returned to civilian and public life.

I recall, in this connection, a little plot in which I was involved around this time. I had suggested to Professor Georg Hohmann, chairman of the Munich Progressive People's Party, that Max Weber be invited for a public lecture. Marianne Weber wrote to me that her husband would do his utmost to beg off. He was still afraid of addressing a large audience, for he had not delivered any public lectures for the past nineteen years. Marianne implored me to hold him fast to the commitment and force him to speak, so that the spell of silence would at last be broken. Herr Hohmann and I then informed Max Weber that cancellation was altogether impossible, and that he must deliver the lecture. As a result, Max Weber appeared on October 27, 1916 at that venerable site of Munich intellectual life called the Mathäserbräu to give his lecture. The title was "Germany and the World Powers"; it has been reprinted in his *Politische Schriften*. He used only a single sheet of notes; I held it in my hand at the time but, alas, could not prevail on him to let me keep it. It consisted of an outline, in his tiny, illegible handwriting, with 1, 2, 3 and 4; a), b), c), d); and he followed this outline with exactitude. It was one of the most magnificent addresses I have ever been privileged to hear. He was a most powerful speaker, as great or perhaps even greater than such celebrated academic lecturers of his time as Lujo Brentano or Ernst Tröltsch or Ulrich von Wilamowitz-Moellendorf. He spoke extemporaneously, merely using this brief outline; and for more than two hours he held the whole audience spellbound.

I should like to read a brief passage that I entered in my diary next day—I ask forbearance for the clumsy prose of a young man. I wrote: "He has become a little grayer; in his beard the gray predominates. His hair, which sits so handsomely around his intellectualized brow, is still thick and abundant. His eyes are deeper-set. When he ponders, his face contracts like the sky before a thunderstorm. It is a manly face; something elemental, at times actually titanic, emanates from him. He speaks freely in his resonant voice, using a magnificently controlled German, every word in its proper relation to the context, and nevertheless it all sounded improvised. His volcanic temperament erupts again and again. But he can also be jocular and turn sardonically humorous. At times, too, there was a surprising coarseness, a hail of words like 'outrageous,' 'shameless,' 'incredible.' It was more of a political sermon than a learned discourse, coming straight from a great, overflowing heart and sustained by a breadth of knowledge and thought that again and again gave something new to us by the very context in which it all was placed. For we are always too much the prey of stale political commonplaces and routine thinking. For two hours a sold-out house listened in breathless suspense."

Those who have not heard him speak cannot imagine the power and expressiveness of his language. I had the good fortune to hear other speeches of his, and especially remember those he delivered in November 1918 during the upheaval in Bavaria (which has been wrongly called a revolution). Again in one of the beerhalls in Munich, standing before a raging crowd, he heaped scorn upon the political literati who were present, though he knew full well that they were the incendiaries of revolution who had already applied the fuse to the powder keg. That was one of his great moments, for he loved to face down opposition. That, too, was the time he drew his famous parallel between the flight of James II from England in 1685 and the undignified flight of the German Kaiser to Holland.

For the Kaiser he had nothing but burning hatred. I myself heard him say several times: "If they would only let me at him, I would personally twist the bungling fool's neck." He considered the Kaiser one of the greatest of Germany's misfortunes in the days of the Second Empire.

There are two more of his lectures that I wish to recall. These were the lectures on "Scholarship as a Profession" and "Politics as a Profession," presented in the Steinicke Hall on Adalbert-strasse in the winter of 1919-1920. Today these must be set among the classic examples of eloquence of the German mind and the German tongue. I shall never forget his saying to us young people in the lecture on "Scholarship as a Profession": "Everything depends on the interpretation of this little passage from Thucydides; my fate and the fate of the world depend on finding the correct interpretation. Only one who has this obsession is a born scholar." But he also knew that scholarship is ephemeral, that it is outmoded after five, ten, at most fifty years, while true art is never surpassed and therefore never outmoded. And in the lecture on "Politics as a Profession," he vividly and with unsparing clarity presented to us, who were filled with a youthful sense of the endless potentialities of a new age, the thorny road of the politician.

After his health had mended still further, and it was known that he was once more available for academic life, he received a whole sheaf of offers. Curiously enough, he accepted the call to Vienna, where his success was absolutely sensational. Hours before his lectures, the audiences would fill the largest auditorium at Vienna University. It reminded me of my own experiences as a student in Paris, where we would go to the Collège de France at nine o'clock in order to hear Henri Bergson at eleven; from nine to ten a valetudinarian lectured on Old Persian, and from ten to eleven someone held forth on Sanscrit—but none of us paid the slightest attention to what they lectured on.

Max Weber used to tell a pretty little anecdote about his Vienna period. One day three very spruce and correctly dressed young men came to his hotel and introduced themselves as the officers of a feudal student association. The conversation went as follows: "Herr Professor, we hear that you are delivering a course of lectures with great success at the University." Max Weber: "That is correct." First officer: "Would it be possible for you to repeat the lectures at our fraternity house if we paid you double the honorarium that the Austrian government pays for lecturing at the University?" Max Weber, raising his eyebrows in astonishment: "But, my dear sirs, all you need to do to hear me is to come to my lectures. You could be sure of seats; as students you have priority." First officer: "Herr Professor, what are you thinking of. Members of our corps can't possibly go to lectures at the University."

A few words about Max Weber's attitude toward youth. He was both kindly and critical. We learned an expression from him that none of us has ever forgotten: intellectual honesty. It meant not going about things with the fuss and to-do of a dilettante. It meant attacking all studies with seriousness, conscientiousness, and pride. It implied the famous three maxims which he left to us and which I should like to recommend to the present younger generation. Number 1: "Crack tough nuts." Anyone can crack the thin-shelled nuts; but a man who has any pride in himself will try to crack only the tough nuts. Number 2: "Be able to meet your routine responsibilities." It is easy to do the exciting and interesting things in life, but extremely hard to submit to the dreary requirements of everyday things that are incumbent upon all of us. And Number 3: "Know how to keep silent." That was what he himself could do least of all. He could not hold his peace. In all the eight years that I knew him, he was forever involved in scholarly and political feuds which he waged with implacable intensity and in which he often fired broadsides that the target did not warrant. He had an innate and inflexible sense of justice that made him take the side of anyone whom he thought was being unjustly dealt with.

Let me finally attempt a sketch, inadequate though it must be, of his personality and a profile of his mind.

First of all, he was a totally unsentimental person. Sentimentality was deeply repugnant to him. He was also a man immune to ideologies. Consequently, he regarded ideologies—

which were then as rampant as they are today—as nothing but more or less accidental facts of a given sociological milieu and by no means as permanent phenomena or metaphysical absolutes. He was against all hero-worship; he called it "idolization of creatures"—today I suppose we would use the term "cult of personality"—and felt it to be intolerable. Yet back of his generally rationalistic attitude he had a profound feeling for true cultural values. He loved and absorbed beauty in life, music, literature, art, architecture, travel, cities, and landscapes.

He was a German patriot. What else could he be? Today he is criticized for attachment to the *Machtstaat,* the power-state. He was indeed attached to it. At the time he saw no other choice. In the years before 1914 and until after the end of the First World War, there were no effective idealistic pacifists or internationalists in Germany or elsewhere in Europe. Max Weber was committed to the idea of the *Machtstaat* because he believed that the German people and German civilization were worth preserving against the rising Slavic tide. He was concerned for what he believed to be Germany's cultural mission in the world. His support of the power-state was not for the benefit of any privileged class. He hated the satiated bourgeoisie. He hated the Junkers; he also had very little respect for the bourgeoisization and bureaucratization of the proletarian leaders. But Germany as a whole represented a real value to him. To charge him with believing in power for its own sake, or with being a forerunner of the horrors of the recent past, is to misunderstand him completely. But he was also a "European" and, in this, far ahead of his time. He regarded the example of England, in particular, as the political, social, and societal ideal, the "ideal type" toward which the Germans should strive with all their might.

Secondly, Max Weber was a daemonic personality. Even in routine matters, there was something incalculable, explosive about him. You never knew when the inner volcano would erupt. He was a foe of all conformity. He was utterly fearless and possessed "civilian courage," as the Germans significantly call it, to a degree that I have never seen in any other German. These very qualities made the party bosses wary, and it is no accident that instead of being nominated to the German National Assembly in Weimar, he was passed over in 1919 in favor of an insignificant party hack. We, his friends, have often wondered what might have become of Germany if Max Weber had obtained the leading position that his personality deserved. At the time we believed that his exclusion from active politics was the greatest mischance that could have befallen Germany. Today I see the matter differently. Given his temperament and his knowledge, he would probably have cut a great figure in political life, but he would have offended so many people that he would have created hosts of enemies. And as for the course of affairs under Weimar, the tragic course of affairs, he would probably have been unable to check it in any way.

In conclusion: he was not only an unsentimental and daemonic personality; he was also the charismatic man that he himself described. He had that exceptional gift of casting his spell upon everyone he encountered. No one who knew him escaped the spell. His disciples and his friends paid him homage. His adversaries paid him respect.

Then the end came. I saw him last on an evening in April or May 1920, at his home on Seestrasse in Munich, together with Marianne and Emil Ludwig and his wife—Ludwig's star was then just beginning to rise; today, for the younger generation, he is already forgotten. That was a highly memorable evening of brilliant conversation. In June I heard he had fallen ill. It was pneumonia, caused by the wave of influenza that swept over the world at that time and took almost as many victims as the war itself. Toward five o'clock one dreary, rainy afternoon I went to the house to ask how he was. Marianne, exhausted from the strain of nursing, had just gone to rest, and Kea took me up to his room, where he lay struggling with death like Jacob with the angel.

During the First World War I had seen many men die, but he was the first I saw dying whom I knew intimately. It was a titanic struggle. I stood there for perhaps ten or fifteen minutes, watching and listening as he fought the Angel of Death. I was, so far as I know, the last person to see him alive. He died shortly after I had left him; I do not believe that Marianne was yet awake. On his deathbed he looked transfigured, emptied of desire, noble as a Hohenstaufen emperor. Later, Marianne sent me a photograph of him on his deathbed. It has hung above my desk for more than forty years.

Then came the funeral service at the Schwabing cemetery. I was to sing a Handel aria to organ accompaniment. Rothenbücher delivered a moving funeral address; Marianne herself spoke; and his favorite pupil, Jörg von Kapherr, talked about the three maxims which I mentioned before as his legacy: cracking tough nuts, meeting routine responsibilities, and knowing how to keep silent.

I have come to the end of my remarks. In a long life that has taken me through many lands, I have known only two human beings whom I should like to call great. One of them was Max Weber, the other Harlan Fiske Stone, Chief Justice of the United States—whom, however, I knew far less well than I did Max Weber. Aside from him, among thousands of encounters, I have never met another who could compare or in any way come up to Max Weber.

Some time ago, before I received the invitation to participate in today's celebration, I read the statement in a respected American magazine that our age has been shaped by the minds of four men, namely Karl Marx, Sigmund Freud, Albert Einstein, and Max Weber. It is an interesting reflection that all four sprang from the German cultural sphere and spoke to the world in the German language. There is no need to say much about

Karl Marx. A third of humanity has been enrolled under his banner. Of Sigmund Freud, we now know that he opened a new dimension to the individual, a new insight into the self, a new kind of self-knowledge. Of Albert Einstein I understand nothing. But I have been told that without him the technological age would be impossible, that he is ultimately responsible for the atomic and electronic age. I think, however, that I do know something about Max Weber. What Freud did for the individual, Max Weber did for the collective. He afforded us insights into the nature, the functioning, and the conduct of those collectivities we call state, city, party, class, and status-group. He revealed to us things we had not seen before in such contexts. What he elucidated, what he left to us as his legacy, has today become part and parcel of our political, social, and scientific thinking to a far greater extent than we ourselves could possibly have realized half a century ago.

When I think of Max Weber, I like to apply to him the words that Cicero used, I believe, of his friend Atticus. He had, Cicero said, four qualities: *auctoritas, urbanitas, labor,* and *industria.* Freely translated, these qualities are: great stature, heartfelt courtesy, incessant effort, unremitting work.

As I have said, no one who met Max Weber could escape the impact of his personality. For me and many others he represented the decisive influence in the formation of our mind.

I am grateful for this occasion to pay tribute to this great man, and so make my own minute contribution to his fame.

Let me close with the words of Goethe on Schiller:

> He shines before us like a comet fleeting,
> Infinitudes of light with his light meeting.

About the Author

Karl Loewenstein has lived and taught in the United States for more than thirty years, and is an expert of international rank in the fields of comparative law and political history. He was born in Munich in 1891, and worked as an attorney-at-law in his home city from 1919 to 1933. At the University of Munich he taught public and international law, and general political theory from 1931 to 1933. In the latter year he emigrated to the United States, spent some years as associate professor of Government at Yale University, and in 1936 was called to Amherst College. There Mr. Loewenstein held the William Nelson Cromwell Chair of Jurisprudence and Political Science for twenty-five years, until his retirement in 1961. During these years he was also visiting professor at the Universities of Colorado, California (Berkeley), Harvard, Yale, Massachusetts, and others. During the last war he was Special Assistant to the Attorney General in Washington, D. C., and was delegated by the U. S. Government to serve as Director of Legislation with an international committee in Uruguay. After the war he served for extended periods as Legal Advisor to the American military government in Germany.

Karl Loewenstein is the author of some fifteen books and ninety articles in the fields of comparative public law and jurisprudence published in six languages. Among them are *Hitler's Germany* (New York, 1939), *Political Reconstruction* (New York, 1946, and *Political Power and the Governmental Process* (Chicago, 1956). Of the last work, containing the *summa* of Professor Loewenstein's lifelong experience with the governmental structure of the past and the present, translations have been published in German, Spanish and Japanese. A number of his articles written in German were collected in the volume, *Beiträge zur Staatssoziologie (Contributions to Political Sociology)*. A large scale treatise on British constitutional law and practice is in the press.

Date Due

Demco 38-297